CONTROLLED
BURN

CONTROLLED BURN

Rising from the Ashes to Forge an Unshakable Faith

BROOKE MARTIN

DEXTERITY
NASHVILLE

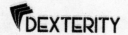

Dexterity, LLC
604 Magnolia Lane, Nashville, TN 37211

Some names and identifying details have been changed to protect the privacy of individuals
whose stories are included in this book.

Printed in the United States of America.
First edition: 2024
10 9 8 7 6 5 4 3 2 1

ISBN: 978-1-962435-10-9 (Paperback)
ISBN: 978-1-962435-11-6 (E-book)
ISBN: 978-1-962435-12-3 (Audiobook)

Publisher's Cataloging-in-Publication Data
Names: Umstattd, Brooke Christine, author.
Title: Controlled burn : rising from the ashes to forge an unshakeable faith / Brooke Martin.
Description: Includes bibliographical references. | Nashville, TN: Dexterity, 2024.
Identifiers: ISBN: 978-1-962435-10-9 (paperback) | 978-1-962435-11-6 (ebook) |
978-1-962435-12-3
(audiobook)
Subjects: LCSH Umstattd, Brooke Christine. | Television news anchors--United States--
Biography. |
Women television journalists--United States--Biography. | Women television news
anchors--United
States--Biography. | Grief--Religious aspects--Christianity. | Christian living. | Christian
biography. |
BISAC BIOGRAPHY & AUTOBIOGRAPHY / Memoirs | BIOGRAPHY &
AUTOBIOGRAPHY / Religious |
RELIGION / Christian Living / Personal Memoirs
Classification: LCC PN4872 .U67 2024 | DDC 070.4/3092--dc23

Cover Design by Dawn Adams/DA Cover Design; Interior design by PerfecType, Nashville, TN

For my sweet Emma Noelle
Until I hold you again . . .

CONTENTS

INTRODUCTION

CRASH OR BURN

It was peaceful up there in the clouds, almost as if we were floating instead of crashing.

The clouds were puffy, cheerful. A beautiful day to die.

"Brooke. I need you to listen *very* carefully. Do you understand?" My pilot's voice snapped me out of my ethereal thoughts. He was urgent and, although one of the most skilled pilots in the world, a little panicked.

"Yes," I shot back with as much confidence as I could muster.

"I need you to put your hands on the ejection pull and when I say, 'Eject,' you need to pull it as hard as you can."

Well, crap.

Being a TV news anchor isn't as glamorous as many think. "Who does your hair?" Yours truly. "Your makeup?"

That's me too. "Where do you get your clothes?" Well, usually, T.J. Maxx, if you must know.

It's a life of deadlines barely met, holidays missed, and late-breaking news. Yet despite the stress and the long hours, TV news is a lot of fun. It also presents some incredible opportunities. Like that time I had to pinch myself while sitting in the Oval Office, asking questions of a sitting US president. Or when, giddy as a kid, I squeezed my tall frame into the tiny second seat of an IndyCar to race around that famed oval with Mario Andretti himself. And I couldn't help but laugh when I stepped onto the court with the Harlem Globetrotters to referee their game. You see, local news might not be glamorous, but for me, it was better. It was adventurous.

So, when my news director told me the Air Force Thunderbirds were coming to town and asked if I wanted to ride with them, I jumped at the chance. It was 2012, in Wichita, Kansas, and I was young and gutsy. After hours of application work, precise body measurements, and medical workups, I realized this would be more than a high-flying joy ride.

I had strict instructions on what *not* to eat that morning and what to drink. I was warned by older photographers at the station that the physicality of this type of flight is demanding, even grueling.

My nerves really started kicking in as my photographer and I pulled into McConnell Air Force Base early that morning and I was presented my flight suit. It fit like a glove. And the small detail of having my name embroidered on the chest somehow made my head grow about five inches. There's no wasting time on an Air Force base, however, so I was quickly ushered into a meeting room for two hours of preflight training. The flight surgeon first explained what my body would be feeling during our time in the air, specifically focusing on when we would pull some Gs. Basically, the pressure causes all the blood in your body to rush to your feet, and it's up to you to try to keep some of it in your head to avoid passing out. To even have a chance at staying conscious, you must do intense breathing and muscle work during the pull. I listened closely, intent on staying alert long enough to hit nine Gs. . . . Bragging rights, I was told.

When the flight surgeon finished, my pilot took over the training, cool as a cucumber. He was a Thunderbirds pilot, after all. He went over the equipment and gear, briefly touching on emergency procedures. "I have to go over this with you, but don't worry." He said it like an inside joke, with a perfunctory "you know how it is" tone.

I chuckled and paid just a little more attention than I give the flight attendants when they're demonstrating how to latch your seat belt before your plane takes off. I had been in my flight suit for just over an hour, and I already thought I owned the world.

Finally, it was time to board, and I walked out to the tarmac, where the coolest plane I had ever seen waited for me. *An F-16 fighter jet.* My heart beat almost as loudly as the engine. As I got closer, I saw my name stenciled on the side of the jet. *My* name. Some people peak in high school; I peaked that beautiful fall day in Wichita. After climbing into the seat behind the pilot, I strapped in and pulled on my helmet and flight mask. I was figuratively on top of the world, and in a few minutes, it was about to be literal.

We hit 450 miles per hour on takeoff and then shot 16,000 feet into the sky. The takeoff alone made my body feel as if it were melting into the seat, so I knew this was about to be insane.

"You ready?" the pilot's voice came through my headset, the scratchy quality reminding me of walkie-talkies.

"Let's do it!" I laughed.

Rolls. Turns. Supersonic engine bursts. The glass cockpit enclosure provided a view unlike anything I had seen, especially considering that a lot of it was upside down.

We were about an hour in, and I still hadn't barfed, which was an accomplishment in and of itself. I started to feel cocky, and I told my pilot we had to hit nine Gs.

"If you're sure!" he said.

So up we shot. Six, seven, eight, nine Gs! I was breathing and contracting all the muscles I could remember from the preflight lesson, and I made it! I was on cloud nine.

Then I started feeling nauseous.

I removed my flight mask and got the barf bag ready. Just as I was telling the pilot I needed to fly straight for a minute, the cockpit screens started flickering. *Weird,* I thought. *But that must be normal. We did just hit nine Gs, after all.*

Suddenly a word started flashing on the screen in front of me. My brow furrowed as I craned my neck to see the same word blinking on the screens in front of the pilot. ERROR! ERROR! ERROR!

"Um . . . ," I began before realizing my pilot was in an urgent conversation with someone else.

Next, the engine went silent, and the cockpit lights went dark. At 16,000 feet in the air.

No. No, no, no was all my brain could muster. Struggling not to panic, I waited for what seemed an eternity for the pilot to address me. Finally, I heard his voice on my headset. "Brooke, I need you to listen very closely. Are you listening?"

"Yes" was all I could eek out.

"I need you to remember what I taught you about emergency procedures."

Seriously!? You said we wouldn't! I screamed in my head.

He told me to get my flight mask back on immediately and never ever, whatever I do, take it off.

"OK, now, turn the knob on the right control board to pure oxygen. Is it there, Brooke?" I remembered something in the training about a toxic chemical used in extreme emergencies. I turned the knob and began breathing pure oxygen.

My pilot went back to his urgent dialogue with traffic control while I sat in the back of a busted F-16 fighter jet that was about to plummet to earth.

Strangely, I felt almost peaceful. Maybe it was the adrenaline or shock, but my fear subsided, and I couldn't stop thinking, *What a way to die.*

I wondered what the headlines might be. "Local anchor dead after fiery Thunderbirds crash." Or maybe they'd go with a cheekier "Anchor drags F-16 to the ground."

I didn't get far into imagining my obituary when another real problem arose. My nose started running. Not dripping. It was *pouring* snot. I don't know if it was the oxygen or if it was my body's way of peeing its pants, but there was nothing I could do. My mask was firmly in place, and I was under strict orders not to remove it for any reason.

The snot didn't stop coming. It quickly rose to my chin. Within a few minutes, it had reached my lips, then covered my mouth. A different, less heroic headline popped into my head: "Local anchor drowns in her own snot."

Another eternity passed before my pilot came back on my headset to ready me for ejection.

As my hands gripped the ejection pull, I waited for his command. Luckily for me, it wasn't needed. The chemical the pilot had deployed allowed the jet's engine to turn enough to float us back to the runway, which I could now see was covered with the flashing lights of emergency vehicles. As we descended for an emergency landing, workers in hazmat suits surrounded the jet. We were alive. The jet was intact. And all of a sudden, bragging rights were not important.

Surrounded by Fire

Although the pilot and I survived that mechanical malfunction, the experience opened my eyes to a reality that went well beyond a newscast: *Life has a way of bringing us down when we least expect it.*

One minute you're flying high, and the next, you're plummeting toward earth at supersonic speed, with error lights flashing. You're panicked, gasping for oxygen, praying this isn't real—but it is.

You receive news of that diagnosis or death.

You've been fired without warning.

You're holding divorce papers in your hand. . . .

They're the devastating crashes of life, the tumultuous storms, the sudden implosions that don't land you safely but instead set your life on fire.

If you've picked up this book, something has probably already happened to you. Something went terribly wrong, and you're in the middle of the wreckage, surrounded by fire, wondering what just happened. You know firsthand that in those times of crisis, it doesn't matter how well you've trained, how skilled you are, or how impressive your plane is—life's crash-and-burns don't discriminate.

This is a hard reality to accept, but if we allow our hearts to see it, a powerful truth coexists with it. Yes, suffering is inevitable, but suffering is also the most profound opportunity we have in this life to truly know God and be transformed by Him. I believe this is why the Bible refers to suffering as fire more than it does to any other imagery. Fire, in its essence, is transformative. Crashes only destroy; storms only ravage; implosions offer no redemption. But if contained, fire holds incredible promise. So does our suffering.

I don't say that lightly as a news anchor with a wild story to tell. I say that as a broken human who, years after that incident in the clouds, would stare death in the face so personally that I thought, even if I went on breathing, it would be the end of me.

I say it because I've walked through its fire, and I'll never be the same.

I say it because I believe, without a shadow of a doubt, that your fire, no matter how devastating, holds the same hope and promise.

DEFYING DARKNESS

Karen Foster surveyed the mountainside. For decades, she had led guests on this same horseback ride almost every week throughout the summer. Her family's ranch was a haven for visitors looking to escape the hustle and bustle of daily life, and the Fosters made it their priority to help guests reconnect with their Creator. But this summer, the summer of 2003, was different.

Many communities in Colorado were still reeling from the aftermath of the worst wildfire in the state's history.

A US Forest Service employee who had burned a letter at a campground had unknowingly set in motion the catastrophic Hayman Fire, which would ultimately claim the lives of five firefighters. The inferno unleashed its wrath upon Pike National Forest, burning more than 138,000 acres and 600 structures. And right in the middle of the mayhem sat Lost Valley Ranch, settled snugly in a valley that earned the Fosters' ranch its name. The lush lowlands, shaped like the back of a hand, were surrounded by the majestic Rocky Mountains. At the forefront of the stunning view lay bright-green pastureland, and beyond that, breathtaking forests, snowcapped mountains, and bright blue sky.

Karen knew which wildflowers grew where and which chirps belonged to which flying friends. But this summer day in 2003, the trail ride felt foreign. Instead of the horses brushing up against towering pines, their riders' knees scraped against charred spindles. Beds of grass and moss had become a mix of dew and ash that created areas of sticky tar. An eerie silence had replaced the once-familiar sounds of birds singing and wildlife scattering. And for my friend Linda, who was on this horseback ride, the smell is what she would never forget. An ungodly stench of smoke and ash—the smell of death itself.

Miraculously, the ranch itself was spared. As if God Himself had drawn a boundary around the entire valley, the flames separated on each side, never touching the ranch's buildings or pastureland. The surrounding mountains, however, had been fair game for the inferno, and those on horseback were getting a firsthand look at the devastation.

As the riders crested a mountainside, their horses' legs covered in black ash, the returning guests within the group were burdened by the devastation. *How is this the same landscape we visit every summer? Will it ever return to its former glory?* Then Karen called their attention to something, gently urging them to look closely.

There, sprouting from beneath the tarry ash, grew tiny flowers. The riders had to force themselves to shift their gaze away from the black canvas. *Look. One, two, three. Pink, purple, yellow.*

How was it even possible? Hundreds of wildflowers were defying death, pushing through the darkness in a daring feat for such delicate creations.

Karen explained to the guests that even with all her wildflower knowledge, she wasn't familiar with this species. It was new to the ranch's landscape. Somehow, someway, the fire's effect had brought these flowers to life, and she would have to learn about them.

Fire Followers

It turns out these flowers have a name: *fire followers.* An actual species of flower whose seeds remain locked within nearly impenetrable shells. These seeds ignore the summoning of sunlight and the encouragement of rainfall. They aren't swayed by the ordinary rhythms of existence. They stay locked away, sometimes for decades, awaiting just one thing.

They demand a fiery furnace of transformation, a searing heat shock that pierces their armor and reveals their life within. Then, after the fire, these seeds grow with amazing speed. The bright-yellow coastal lotus reaches skyward, stunning its black canvas background. The twining snapdragon wraps itself around the charred skeletons of other shrubs, decorating the dead branches with delicate purple blooms.

The plants are testaments of perseverance. Of beauty from the ashes. They're pictures of what's possible. They're surprising—a seemingly new addition to a landscape—when all along, their seeds have been there, just waiting for fire to bring them to life.

Right now, deposited deep within your soul, are fire followers. Seeds of truth, revelation, and power awaiting a heat shock to unlock them. These seeds, lovingly sown by your Creator, have perhaps been lying dormant your whole life. But it's in the heat of suffering that the Holy Spirit, the Spirit of God, cracks open their shells and cultivates something extraordinary, a kind of beauty that puts any flower to shame. The heat produces a profound awareness of God's presence and an assurance of His astonishing love.

A Vision from the Fire

I was still digging through the ash of my own landscape one summer day. It had been two years since our daughter's death, and I was trying to understand a new and debilitating anxiety that was visiting me with increasing regularity. The sun was shining brightly through my windshield as I drove down I-65 South, Indianapolis's Lafayette Road the latest exit to shrink in my rearview mirror. This was the same route I had taken every day to work for eight years, but today was different. I had decided to take an extended leave from my job because of this increasing anxiety, and for the first time in my adult life, I wouldn't be anchoring the nightly news.

I knew it wasn't good, this foreign feeling that was creeping up and invading my life. For the better part of the previous year, I'd had the curious sense of being nudged away from the career I'd spent most of my life building. A career I was good at, and one that lent me credibility, recognition, and respect.

Now that gentle nudge was turning into an uncomfortable pull, and my anxiety was only increasing. Not one to abandon lifelong goals easily, I did the only thing I knew to do as I drove. "God," I prayed, "if You are calling me out of news, please tell me what You're calling me into."

Then I saw it—an image so clear for having been nonexistent just a moment before. I blinked, trying to keep my eyes on the road while also seeking to decipher the scene that was playing somewhere behind my eyes. It was a burned-out forest, but not one I had ever actually seen. Charred stumps dotted the ground. Black spindles barely stood where trees had once towered. Mounds of ash covered the landscape. The image was followed with two words that, although inaudible, I clearly understood: *controlled burn.*

This was my life in full view. And there was no denying it.

My husband and I were still trying to make sense of our loss. It had been two years since we watched our baby girl take her last breath. Two years of an unrecognizable landscape. Two years of trying to see through the lingering smoke.

It had also been two years of sensing the gentle breeze of hope. Two years of reorienting my view without the tall evergreens to block certain vistas. This uncharted territory, although terrifying at times, was swirling with a powerful force propelling me to venture further into my new landscape.

This vision and those two words—*controlled burn*—would begin a divine conversation. From that point on, I didn't do much talking. Instead, I listened as God started revealing the potential of life's fires, if only I would have perspective. The perspective that my suffering didn't have to be some raging wildfire over which I was powerless, but rather, my suffering could be a controlled burn. A transformative act calling me out of mere survival and into a new reality with Jesus. A containment of my pain, bordered by purpose and promise, where the flames could burn what was keeping me away from God and spur new life and growth that could never have sprouted otherwise.

In response to my plea for what was next, God didn't directly answer my question. I asked for instruction, and instead, He handed me an invitation. He was revealing a new path, one that could only emerge from the pain of flames. A trail so unfamiliar, I knew I couldn't walk it alone . . . nor was I being asked to. I didn't fully understand it then, but in my pain I knew God was beckoning me to something more, something new.

Harnessing Heat

I began doing what a journalist does: I researched controlled burning. I discovered the act to be almost as ancient as fire itself.

Back in the mists of time, our earliest ancestors contained flames to drive game into traps and to clear away dry brush. As human civilization evolved and spread across the globe, so did the practice of controlled burning. From the ancient Greeks and Romans to the Native Americans of North America and the Aboriginal peoples of Australia, cultures around the world have recognized the value of harnessing fire in this way.

It seems counterintuitive at first glance. Igniting perfectly fine terrain? Yet the purposes of a controlled burn are profound. This singular act can restore an entire landscape's ecosystem. It can clear a forest of dry brush that, were it to be hit with a single lightning strike, would fuel a devastating wildfire. It can rid land of the most invasive of species.

These deliberate fires (sometimes referred to as *prescribed fires*) are a delicate dance of chaos and order, destruction and renewal. There is no room for recklessness, and no denial of what's lost in the process. Careful consideration is taken with every aspect, from drawing the boundary lines to deciding on the accelerant to carefully monitoring weather conditions and timing the ignition. Nothing is overlooked; no detail is too small to ignore, because the outcome is worth the risk.

It turns out that the risk is minimal. According to the US Forest Service, its prescribed fire program has a 99.84 percent success rate.[1] God can guarantee even better. Psalm 119:50 offers us this: "Your promise revives me; it comforts me in all my troubles" (NLT). That word "all" means *all*, every time. Yes, some details of any fire are unpredictable, and yes, every single flame burns, but it's the outcome of a controlled burn that compels the ranger to light the torch.

Imagine the absurdity, the danger, of igniting a controlled burn with only slight confidence that it would do any good or stay contained. If we don't have the promise within our suffering, the notion of hope is just as absurd and perhaps even more dangerous.

The Sustaining Promise

Every person to walk this earth will inevitably encounter personal fire, and from the outside looking in, it all resonates similarly as heartache, grief, or pain. Much as flames retain their inherent nature whether they're inside a wildfire or in a controlled burn, our suffering holds universal similarities from one person to another.

What truly distinguishes both a controlled burn and the suffering of the children of God from a raging wildfire is the promise that sustains them—the hope that permeates the fire. Hope whispers of things to come, of a changing landscape. Hope's very existence is precisely why the Bible tells us we are not to grieve like the rest of the world, which grieves without hope (1 Thessalonians 4:13).

I want to be clear here to acknowledge that suffering is not inherently valuable in itself. Rather, the transformative power of God's grace, and His promise of eternal glory, give profound significance and perspective to our pain.

An Intimate Invitation

Sadhu Sundar Singh was an Indian Christian missionary from the early 1900s who knew suffering. Although he was born into a Sikh family, his mother enrolled him in a British missionary school to learn English. Sundar was neither convinced nor comforted by the answers the priests provided, so he studied Hindu beliefs. Yet his own religious pursuits left him empty as well.

One day, at age fourteen, his life crashed and burned when his mother died. Consumed with anger, the teenager burned a Bible page by page. A few nights later, a restless and lost Sundar awoke and prayed that the true God would appear to him; otherwise, he had resolved to take his own life.

That very night, he had a vision of Jesus.

Sundar committed his life to following this Jesus he had heard so much about, but the costs were enormous. First, he was disowned by his father and poisoned by his brother. Later, he was persecuted by many others and often imprisoned as he traveled and preached. Nevertheless, he spent his life serving the sick and bringing the gospel to some of the remotest parts of the world.

He was sustained in part by an experience that gave him enduring perspective. Singh wrote:

> One day after a long journey, I rested in front of a house. Suddenly a sparrow came towards me blown helplessly by a strong wind. From another direction, an eagle dived to catch the panicky sparrow. Threatened from different directions, the sparrow flew into my lap. By choice, it would not normally do that. However, the little bird was seeking for a refuge from a great danger. Likewise, the violent winds of suffering and trouble blow us into the Lord's protective hands.[2]

Whether you've endured the agonizing flames for years or are just witnessing the first flicker, what will rise from the ashes depends on your perspective on pain and your heart's posture toward possibility. As the late pastor and theologian Timothy Keller said, "There is a purpose to [suffering], and if faced rightly, it can drive us like a nail deep into the love of God and into more stability and spiritual power than you can imagine."[3]

Do you dare believe it?

Right now, as the embers flare, you are being handed an invitation. The smoke may be too thick for you to see it clearly, and that's OK. But it's an invitation that is personally and intimately *for you*.

I remember when I began to decipher the significance of my own invitation. In the aftermath of my fire, I often received words of encouragement about what lies ahead: eternity with God, where all things will be made new; a splendor in which sorrow and pain become mere echoes of a distant past; a place where death itself is a forgotten memory.

It's a breathtaking reality that awaits every believer, and while I cherished the encouragement, that wasn't what God was beckoning me to. My invitation was an awakening—a deep realization that in the here and now, in the problems and the pain, lies my only chance to share in the sufferings of Jesus Himself. I was beginning to understand that, this side of heaven, my broken heart is the most intimate offering I can give my dearest Friend and Savior. My invitation was not to look past my circumstances or try to rush through them, but to gaze at the face of Jesus in the midst of them.

What I'm saying may seem unfathomable to you right now. Maybe you've just watched your marriage go up in flames, or you're witnessing the daily decline—the slow smoldering—of someone you love due to addiction, a terminal illness, or dementia. Maybe you adored a person who has ended his or her own life, and you're trying to find your way through the shock and the shifting haze of emotions. Maybe you wake up in the middle of the night, hoping that your diagnosis was just a bad dream.

I know how real, how excruciating, the fire is. No words can reverse its impact. It is burned into our memories, irrevocably changing our lives. But the landscape left behind isn't what it seems at first glance. There are things to be explored . . . uncovered . . . understood . . . made new.

It can be daunting to even consider the notion of hope from a fire. With this book, I do want to encourage and console you when the fires of life erupt, but my paramount goal is to lead you through the wasteland to the lookout point where hope and promise are clearly seen.

I pray that in this moment you begin to believe there are miracles waiting ahead if you will grasp Jesus's scarred hand and walk into the fire with faith. The choice is yours, but the promise is His. When you and I allow God to guide us through the flames, we can emerge from the other side forged and fearless.

IMAGINE: Look. Closer. From the depths of the ash that covers your landscape, in the dark unseen recesses of your heart, what fire followers do you sense God wants to unlock within you? Do you even believe new growth is possible? As we begin this journey of your controlled burn, let honesty lead the way. Do you cautiously embrace the curiosity of what is being cultivated underneath the ruin? Or do you feel as dead inside as the foliage surrounding you? No question, doubt, or emotion has to be buried. Just as a tiny seed doesn't require the strength of the sower to sprout and flourish, God doesn't need your performance or perfection to unleash profound hope amid your pain. It's a force of nature as unstoppable as the wildflowers that rise through the scorched forest floor, breathing new life into the ashes of yesterday.

2

OUR TRUE TOPOGRAPHY

A powerful gospel truth lies beneath our controlled burn analogy, but we must dig deep to find it. This truth is not found in the motivation or consolation we sometimes gain through suffering, as significant as those discoveries can be. Rather, it's a truth I wish I had understood at the spark of my life's biggest fire: that God is at work in our pain more than we can possibly imagine.

Our lives, just like a forest, can receive fire in one of two ways: as a victim of scorched-earth destruction or as the recipient of opportunity and redemption. To accomplish the latter, we must begin with a walk through our forests. We must observe what's growing and how it got there. We must start at the beginning . . .

In the Beginning

In everything, but especially in pain, we must unfurl ourselves from the tight knot of our current reality and reorient our focus. It's so easy to curl up and lose our bearings in the darkness of our valleys, isn't it? The veil of suffering can blind us to what we foundationally need: truth.

You may not *feel* as though you need truth beneath you, but it's critical in countless ways. You see, truth doesn't change from one day to the next. It cannot be swayed by popular opinion or the wind currents of culture. It's steadfast and resolute. More important, God Himself is truth. When a fire ignites in your life, you will likely be offered temporary relief and speculative answers to the deepest questions of your soul. You might be tempted to seek quick and easy solutions. But I urge you, don't settle.

In the face of suffering, coffee-mug encouragement will not suffice, and not even the most impressive wisdom from the world can apply enough pressure to stop a bleeding heart. We need something far greater. We need the assurance of timeless, unbiased truth. Through bleary eyes, it lets us see more clearly. In heartbreak, we are able to view the whole picture.

As we begin this metaphorical journey through our controlled burn, you and I must, first and foremost, understand who is in control of it. We need to know: *Can God be trusted?* Then we need to walk with the Creator Himself through the intricate forests of our souls.

What's growing in our individual forests can range from God's deliberate design to inadvertent or willful sin. Some of the dense branches may stem from past trauma. Our suffering acts as the fire, and what is brought forth as a result . . . is to be discovered. First, though, let's return to our genesis and understand who God is and who we are. We know ourselves to be sinners, but as we muster the courage to realign our focus on Him and see ourselves as God sees us—stunning creations, reflections of His divine image—we will discover the trail leading to healing and hope.

Who God Is

Thankfully, we are graced with an unmistakable guidepost from the very first verse in the very first chapter of the Bible. "In the beginning, God . . ." We're so familiar with this phrasing that we can easily become immune to its significance. Notice it doesn't read, "In the beginning, you . . ." or "In the beginning, we . . ."

No. "In the beginning, *God* created the heavens and the earth" (Genesis 1:1, emphasis mine).

In the beginning—while the earth was without form and void, while darkness was over the face of the deep, eons before your existence—was God, the Creator of everything. He created day and night—everything we see and everything we don't. He created the waters and the land—everything we understand about this world and everything we don't. He created the heavens, the spiritual realms that are filled with His glory (Genesis 1:2–24; Psalm 19:1)—a place where He is exalted (Psalm 148:13).

Imagine it. A place where a multitude of angels carry out His will (Hebrews 1:14), where cherubim and seraphim continually worship and serve Him (Isaiah 6:2–3; Ezekiel 10:1–22); a throne room surrounded by heavenly beings, saints, and believers (Revelation 4:2–11).

This is beauty beyond our imaginations, majesty that would melt us, and holiness that is reserved for one only: one true God, one Savior of the world.

Everything we know and can even imagine started with God, exists in God, is being executed by God, and will end in eternity with God for those who believe.

Eternity itself is an attribute of God: "Lord, you have been our dwelling place in all generations," reads Psalm 90:1.

Psalm 90 is one of the most poignant passages in Scripture regarding the eternity of God. Its writer, an Israelite named Moses, had been through a lot. Born into peril and rescued, Moses was raised by the very people who oppressed his own bloodline for generations. Taking a stand as a young man, he killed a ruthless Egyptian slave master and spent forty years in exile.

God's call from a burning bush thrust Moses from exile into a position of leadership he never wanted. The Lord sent Moses back to his childhood home to demand freedom for the Israelites, a people chosen by God Himself.

Pharaoh, the ruler of Egypt, wavered, and the Egyptians paid the devastating consequences in the form of ten plagues. Eventually, Moses's plea for the long-awaited liberation of God's people was granted, only to be followed by decades of wandering in the wilderness as they journeyed toward a land God had promised them. Forty years after leaving Egypt, the Israelites entered the promised land, a land Moses would never himself live in. In one especially grievous time, Moses implored God, "Blot me out of your book that you have written" (Exodus 32:32).

Reading his story, it's obvious that Moses knew pain. He knew loss. He knew loneliness. Yet through it all, Moses maintained a confidence that was vital to his survival, and he expressed it in Psalm 90:2: "Before the mountains were brought forth, or ever you had formed the earth and the world, from everlasting to everlasting you are God."

With these verses, Moses was building his case on a foundation that will not fail. He then framed it on the understanding that man, in fact, will fail. "The years of our life are seventy, or even by reason of strength eighty; yet their span is but toil and trouble" (v. 10).

After rightly ordering God's eternity and our temporal existence, Moses didn't plead for the suffering to end. He implored God to help us "get it," to give us understanding to see the bigger picture: "So teach us to number our days that we may get a heart of wisdom" (v. 12).

Moses's words reveal the truth we must absorb deep in our souls: humans were made for God, not the other way around. He created us; we don't get to create our ideal God. God says of humanity, "I have made them *for my glory*. It was I who created them" (Isaiah 43:7 NLT, emphasis mine).

In the Gospel of Luke, we read of a time when, after Jesus had finished praying, His disciples asked, "Lord, teach us to pray." Jesus responded with what we know today as the Lord's Prayer, which, for many of us, has become so recognizable that it's been voided of its power (11:1–4). But just zero in on Jesus's first line: "Our Father in heaven, hallowed be Your name" (v. 2 NKJV). Jesus was telling His disciples to begin their prayers by acknowledging God in

His rightful place. *God! You're in heaven! I'm not! You are holy, Father!*

Different translations say, "Father, your name be honored as holy" (CSB) and "Our heavenly Father, may the glory of your name be the center on which our life turns" (TPT). Our constant, our bedrock, must always be that He is God. In our joy, in our sorrow, in our abundance, and in our lack, this life is not about us. These days that have been ordained to us are not about us. All of this is of Him, by Him, and for Him.

Who We Are

It's the outrageous finale of creation. After all the unspeakable glory God formed from nothing—after the billions of galaxies and innumerable creatures of the sea, after the snow-topped mountains kissed the clouds, after the majestic waves were taught how far to roll—the God of the universe crowned His creation with the one creation that is made in His image—us: "So God created man in his own image, in the image of God he created him; male and female he created them. And God blessed them. And God said to them, 'Be fruitful and multiply and fill the earth and subdue it, and have dominion over the fish of the sea and over the birds of the heavens and over every living thing that moves on the earth'" (Genesis 1:27–28).

In the intricate design of existence, we see God's desire. He desires to be with us.

It's easy to skim over this profound notion and jump right to Adam and Eve's doomed disobedience, but we cannot miss our ordained position in God's grand design. It's huge. Far too frequently, we accrue all of God's love to Jesus and what He did to redeem us from the consequences of sin. But let's endeavor to fathom the love of the Father here, as it manifests in creation. We must try to see ourselves as God sees us; otherwise, when the fire is raging, His promises will be difficult to believe. They'll resonate as mere folklore rather than as the transformative truths they truly are.

I say this because, as modern-day Christians, most of us are well aware of our faults. We grasp with clarity our need for a Savior. But it's a different story when it comes to acknowledging our divine design. If we don't outright avoid that truth, we hesitate to admit it. For example, when was the last time you exclaimed, "Body and soul, I am marvelously made!"? I don't know about you, but my answer is somewhere in the span of . . . never.

Somehow an acknowledgment of our shortcomings feels safer, doesn't it? Yet those words—more precisely, "I am fearfully and wonderfully made"—are the exact words David penned in Psalm 139:14. Read the other psalms he wrote, and it's clear that David also understood and acknowledged his flaws. Yet he didn't allow his weaknesses to obscure his sense of God's profound love for him. *He was vulnerable in both his brokenness and his beauty.* You and I can be too.

One well-known biblical figure with a sordid past was Paul. If anyone had reason to skim over God's love, it was the guy who had persecuted and imprisoned God's own people for a living! Yet in a letter to the church in ancient Ephesus, Paul, in explaining the staggering concept of God's love for us through Jesus Christ, referred to us as God's "workmanship" (Ephesians 2:10). In Greek, the word is *poema*, which we translate as "poem."

You are God's poem. *You.*

Take stock of how that makes you feel. Grateful? Awkward? Surprised?

Your ultimate identity is found in your Creator. You have been fashioned by His loving hands. He is the One who knit you in your mother's womb and designed you with unique gifts and talents reflecting who He is. So, the next time you look in the mirror, you can confidently say, "I have my Father's eyes." When you crack a joke that lands perfectly, take delight in the fact that your sense of humor comes from Him. And when you create something beautiful, acknowledge that your talent is a glimpse of His creativity. You are not defined by your genetics or your circumstances. You are designed with a purpose and infused with God's love. God made you because He loves you.

This is vulnerable stuff—internalizing the intimacy with which God loves us. But unless each of us understands this critical piece, our interaction with God will inevitably resemble the perfunctory exchanges we have with our bank teller: mere transactions marked by pleasantries or judgmental glances, depending on the day.

Where Love Leads

In the moving children's book *You Are Special*, Max Lucado spins a curious tale about a community of wooden figures known as Wemmicks. All day long, the Wemmicks spend their hours affixing golden star stickers to one another for qualities they admire and gray dots for things they disapprove of. One particularly downtrodden and dot-covered Wemmick, Punchinello, is amazed when he encounters a fellow villager who bears no stickers at all. Lucia explains her secret: "Every day I go see Eli." Punchinello peers up the hill to where Eli the woodcarver's workshop sits. After wrestling with the decision, Punchinello decides to go see him too. Punchinello is shocked when Eli welcomes him by name.

"You know my name?" the little Wemmick asks.

"Of course I do. I made you." Eli stoops down, picks him up, and sets him on his workbench. Looking at the gray dots, he speaks thoughtfully: "Hmm. Looks like you've been given some bad marks."

Punchinello tries to defend himself, but Eli says, "All that matters is what I think. And I think you are pretty special."

Punchinello laughs. "'Me, special? Why? I can't walk fast. I can't jump. My paint is peeling. Why do I matter to you?"

Eli looks at Punchinello, puts his hands on those small wooden shoulders, and says very slowly, "Because you're mine. That's why you matter to me."[1]

Never once have I been able to read those words without a great big lump lodging in my throat. Why is it, I wonder, that as grown-ups, we tend to squash down our longing, our hunger, for love? We get tangled up in the bustle of our day-to-day activities or focused on the fires in our lives; all the while, our hearts are craving one thing above all else: connection with our Creator. A gentle nudge that reminds us we belong to Him. A knowing glance assuring us that He is good and that we are loved beyond measure.

Way back in the day, theologian and philosopher Augustine of Hippo said something profound. He said that God created us for Himself, and that our hearts are always going to be restless until we find our rest in Him.[2] I don't know about you, but that hits me in the gut. I think it's because Augustine's words offer a kind of comfort. They remind each of us, *I'm not alone in my longing, and there is, in fact, an answer to it.*

Pain with Purpose

Why is it so crucial we understand God's love for us? Because a right understanding of His love will supernaturally release submission in our hearts as a dandelion releases its seeds to the wind. A realization of His love will create a desire to yield and a yearning to surrender—attitudes that are contrary to our human nature. The apostle Paul reminds us, "The mind governed by the flesh is hostile to God; it does not submit to God's law, nor can it do so" (Romans 8:7 NIV). He was saying that it's impossible to submit ourselves into loving God; we can only be loved into submission.

OK, then, why does submission matter? Ah, here it is. We can't miss this. It matters because *submission is the crucial difference between pain that is pointless and pain that has purpose.* Submission is Jesus Christ's example to us all—submission to our heavenly Father.

> Have this attitude in yourselves which was also in Christ Jesus, who, although He existed in the form of God, did not regard equality with God a thing to be grasped, but emptied Himself, taking the form of a [servant], and being made in the likeness of men. . . . He humbled Himself by becoming obedient to the point of death, even death on a cross. *For this reason* also, God highly exalted Him, and bestowed on Him the name which is above every name. (Philippians 2:5–9 NASB1995, emphasis mine)

No matter what we think of it, submission isn't a demotion. It's a right understanding of who God is and who we are. It's a posture from which God can lay incredible purpose upon you. That's not a demotion. It's an invitation to the most fulfilling existence possible.

Disoriented DNA

We must constantly realign our perspective to God because disorientation is in our DNA. We are sons of Adam and daughters of Eve. Our first ancestors were the only humans who knew what it was like to experience intimacy with the Creator, untainted by sin. They were the only people to ever get to marvel in His majesty unbound by insecurity, false assumptions, judgment, or shame. Adam and Eve lived in perfect innocence in a perfect paradise filled with beautiful plants, gentle animals, and plentiful food. They were never wanting. They savored a close relationship with God, walking and talking with Him in the cool of the day. No worries, no concerns, just one rule: "Do not eat from the tree of the knowledge of good and evil—or you will die" (see Genesis 2:15–17).

We all know what happened. Satan tempted Eve by saying, "You will not surely die. For God knows that when you eat of it your eyes will be opened, and you will be like God, knowing good and evil." And when she "saw that the tree was good for food, and that it was a delight to the eyes, and that the tree was to be desired to make one wise, she took of its fruit and ate, and she also gave some to her husband who was with her, and he ate" (3:4–6).

Eve had everything she could ever have needed or wanted, but the enemy convinced her she wanted something she was never made to handle: the knowledge of good and evil. Just as Satan had said, Adam and Eve's eyes were opened, but what did they realize? All the secrets of the universe? No. They realized they were naked. And *they* decided that was bad.

This knowledge they were never meant to have made them anxious and self-absorbed. Right away, they began to make judgments. Right away, they started assessing, *How do we do damage control? Better yet, how do we fix this?*

What was Adam and Eve's solution to the "fire" they had just ignited in their garden? They got to work sewing fig leaves together and hiding from God. God came along and asked, "Where are you?" and Adam responded, "I heard the sound of you in the garden, and I was afraid, *because I was naked,* and I hid myself" (vv. 7–10, emphasis mine).

Do you see what's happening in this story? Once sin is introduced into the human psyche, a disoriented Adam doesn't claim to be afraid because he disobeyed. Adam says he's afraid because of something that was never designed to be wrong: his nakedness. For the first time ever, Adam and Eve are focused on themselves and not God. They're deciding what's right and wrong. They're determining the best way to deal with shame and, more broadly, the damage of sin.

The Big Questions

This desire for the knowledge of good and evil has followed humanity ever since. To this day, you and I are still desperate to reason our way through the fire and fix what we cannot fix. In suffering, we try to understand things our minds were never created to comprehend. We strive to elevate our understanding and cradle our questions. We are quick to draw lines between good and evil and assess what God should or shouldn't allow. All the while, we are missing out on the one thing we need most in life and in our pain: God's presence.

Instead of letting our life circumstances draw us closer to God, we hide. Not behind literal trees, but behind our own determinations and solutions.

Ultimately, we face a choice. *We can go after God's presence, or we can go after proof.* Here's the difference: You know you're in the presence of God when there's an exchange. You bring Him your shame, pain, or brokenness, and He exchanges it for His joy, comfort, and peace. Sometimes you'll get some form of an answer, but His greatest gift is Himself and the purpose He provides. With Him, you are never left staring into the void.

Proof, on the other hand, offers no exchange; it only elicits more questions, leaving us more lost, more exposed to the heat. Proof is a monster whose appetite only grows, ravenous for confusion. Proof is the serpent in the garden, whispering half-truths while sowing doubt and deception. And the relentless pursuit of proof at any cost will lead to a slow spiritual death.

I want to clearly state that questions are not the culprit. It is entirely normal and reasonable to have questions. God encourages you and me to bring Him our genuine and unfiltered thoughts and to engage our intellect and reason. There's nothing wrong with wrestling with a question. Just make sure you're honest with yourself about your objective.

Are you seeking proof of His goodness before you fully trust Him? Are you allowing your feelings of injustice to render truth inconsequential? Are you demanding evidence of His existence?

Or . . . are you surrendering? Are you coming out from behind the tree, naked and vulnerable, admitting, *I don't know everything, but I do know I want to be with You?* Are you willing to exchange your perceived rights and claims to "understanding" for proximity with Him?

At some point, our worship has to outweigh our worry, and our desire to be in God's presence must surpass our determination to resolve the mysteries of the fire.

Our Colossal God

I know there are significant questions about pain and suffering. Believe me: I've asked them. And I want to tell you I've found the answers.

I want to tell you God will never give you more than you can handle.

I want to tell you God never causes your suffering; He only allows it.

I want to tell you that whatever you think should be true about God, is true. . . .

But God is so much more than clichés and too powerful to be put in simple, feel-good boxes. We're talking about a God who is completely just *and* loving, holy *and* compassionate—100 percent of the time. The God who flooded the earth and who now promises our rule and reign over it in eternity. The God who in anger plagued the Egyptians with boils and who in mercy healed one man with leprosy. The God who invited Satan to test Job and who then defeated Satan once and for all on a wooden cross. The God who shockingly turned Lot's wife into a pillar of salt and then, just as shockingly, rewarded the faith of a Roman centurion. The God who struck Ananias and Sapphira dead for lying and then used the man who had denied Him three times to spread the gospel of the kingdom of heaven to all who would believe.

There is no box big enough, no comprehension capable enough, no justification just enough. There is only one truth: God is God. We are not. And regardless of what we can do or understand or want to believe, God is still sitting on the throne of heaven right now. And even in suffering, He is sovereign. And especially in grief, He is close.

This truth of His supremacy should serve as the most healing of balms to the wounded heart. This means we can rest in His omnipotence. We can submit our questions, doubts, and beliefs to the One who is unrivaled. We can express our longings, anger, and pain to this almighty God whose love is so colossal it conquered death. We can trust in this heavenly Father whose forgiveness runs so deep it drowns even the most heinous sin of the one who repents.

"That sounds nice, but it isn't fair," you might say. But the concept of fairness is a complete falsity. If we can't believe in a God who would allow suffering, we can't believe in a God who would send His one and only Son to die on our behalf.

Fairness cannot be our plumb line. Fairness will fail us every single time. We need something far greater. C. S. Lewis said it this way:

> The problem of reconciling human suffering with the existence of a God who loves, is only insoluble so long as we attach a trivial meaning to the word "love," and look on things as if man were the centre of them. Man is not the centre. God does not exist for the sake of man. Man does not exist for his own sake. "Thou hast created all things, and for thy pleasure they are and were created" (Rev. 4:11). We were made not primarily that we may love God (though we were made for that too) but that God may love us, that we may become objects in which the Divine love may rest "well pleased."[3]

Rightly ordering God's place in eternity and ours will be our bedrock, the firm ground for our controlled burn. When the smoke starts rising, when the flames grow, we will return to this faultless foundation, remembering that in the sovereign God's hands—within His boundaries and His ability to turn evil into redemption—there is a plan and a purpose.

Remembering that even the most raging inferno is within His control.

Remembering that He loves us and longs to be with us.

IMAGINE: Take a moment to close your eyes and let your mind wander through the expanse of your own woodland. Picture it vividly—the mighty trees reaching to the sky. What types of trees populate the landscape? Strong oak? Towering redwoods? Beautiful aspens or birches?

What do you hear? Murmurs of nearby water? A babbling brook? A rushing waterfall? The screech of a red-tailed hawk?

What do you smell? Earthy grass? Wild honeysuckle? Clean pine? Embrace the untamed beauty that resides in your heart, for it is here where you, like Adam and Eve, can walk in the cool of the day with your Creator. It is here where you understand, without a shadow of a doubt, that you are known and deeply, deeply loved. Together, we continue on this sacred expedition.

3

A SURVEY OF THE LANDSCAPE

Did young Philipp Franz von Siebold ever daydream about his name gracing the pages of history books?

I wonder.

As fate would have it, he did indeed leave his mark. Just not for the reason anyone dreams. In the year 1850, during a voyage to the exotic shores of Japan, Siebold became captivated by a plant unlike any he had ever seen. He just knew, with its unique bamboo-like stems and heart-shaped leaves, it would be the talk of the United Kingdom's gardening elites. Excitedly, he brought *Fallopia japonica*, or Japanese knotweed, to England, and it turned out he was right. Gardeners clamored to add Japanese knotweed to their landscapes. Seemingly overnight, the plant became the darling of ornamental cultivation.

But as time passed, the knotweed revealed its true nature. From this seemingly innocent introduction grew, quite literally, the most invasive and destructive plant species to ever take root. Its once-admired qualities, like its rapid growth and ability to thrive in varied environments, quickly became the very things that unleashed ecological and economic mayhem. After escaping the confines of English gardens, the Japanese knotweed soon engulfed all of Europe and beyond, initiating new colonies from the tiniest fragments of its roots or stems. Eradication became impossible.

The weed conquered riverbanks and cracked roads, and it infiltrated houses and infrastructure alike. The mere sighting of knotweed on a property would plummet its value. To this day, although more managed, the fight against the Japanese knotweed continues.

The Root Issues

It isn't lost on me that when sin entered the world, so did weeds. "Cursed is the ground because of you," God told Adam. "In pain you shall eat of it all the days of your life; thorns and thistles it shall bring forth for you" (Genesis 3:17–18).

Weeds and sin share common traits: both grow quickly, are stubborn, and can be deceptively attractive. You may be thinking, *OK, that's true, but why talk about sin while we're already processing pain?* It might seem strange or even cruel, but stay with me, because the reasons are significant.

First, *nothing can eradicate sin like suffering.* Even the most stubborn strongholds cannot escape the flames when the fire of pain roars through. Pain burns away our pretense and strips us of strength to posture. Our sin lies exposed, vulnerable to the refining fires of suffering. For us to pursue hope and healing in our suffering, we have to acknowledge the very things God desires to purify us of through it. If we don't, then to pursue healing is like undergoing liposuction while downing a carton of ice cream—the procedure may work for a time, but unless it's paired with a transformed lifestyle, the pain and the promise that come with it will go to waste.

Of course, this is not to say that pain eliminates all sin in our lives forever, but there's a reason the Bible consistently credits the fires of life as transformative: They bring us to the end of ourselves. They expose our vulnerabilities and help us recognize our need for the unwavering strength of God Himself.

The second reason for discussing sin in the middle of the pain is that *if left unchecked, sin will choke out the hope we need above all else in times of suffering—the hope of Jesus Christ.* His hope is powerful. It is the anchor of our souls, whispering to us of joy on the horizon and assuring us of

God's promises. But unrepentant sin will smother hope, transforming our sorrow into despair. Despair is simply grief without hope.

Third, *unaddressed sin will fuel additional fires or can prolong the one we're in.* In this sense, to carefully identify and root out sin serves as either: (1) a great form of fire prevention, or (2) an important element of a current controlled burn.

Forest ecologists know that controlled burns are extremely effective in preventing future wildfires and limiting the size of any that might start. Controlled burns rid a landscape of tinder-ready fuel, like dry brush, dead trees, and overgrown thickets. Consequently, these controlled burns dramatically decrease the likelihood of a far more catastrophic wildfire in the future. In much the same way, our current pain has the potential to clear our lives of stubborn sin that, were it otherwise ignored, could contribute to other suffering down the road.

Even amid an already-raging controlled burn, sin can prolong the pain. Resentment, the desire for revenge, the haunting grip of despair—they all vie for a chance to stoke the flames and extend our agony. Instead of allowing God's healing truth to tend to our hearts, we can become fixated on blaming others or numbing ourselves. These root issues can fuel our flames for decades, even a lifetime.

Simple and Deadly Serious

Sin was introduced at the start of creation, and it has barreled through generations ever since. Cain's murder of his brother, Jacob's theft of a birthright, the Pharisees' hypocrisy, my jealousy, your pride—this spiritual weed is pervasive and insidious. The great preacher Charles Spurgeon once said, "As the salt flavours every drop in the Atlantic, so does sin affect every atom of our nature. It is so sadly there, so abundantly there, that if you cannot detect it, you are deceived."[1]

If you and I think of sin merely as that bad habit we just can't seem to kick or the white lie we should not have told, we're missing the reality. Nothing is more deadly serious than sin, and few things simpler. *Sin is anything that separates us from God.* In God's presence, despite any circumstance, we find freedom both here on earth and in eternity. But sin threatens that presence.

Consider for a moment the current state of affairs in our world. Every affliction that plagues humans today, from political corruption and religious abuse to physical pain and disease, can be traced back to some kind of sin. And let me assure you, God is angry about it.

God's anger about the brokenness in this world proves His unwavering justice—but also how much He cares. Bible scholar N. T. Wright explains, "It is because God loves the glorious world he has made and is utterly determined to put everything right that he is utterly opposed to everything that spoils or destroys that creation, especially the human creatures who were supposed to be the linchpins of his plan for how that creation would flourish."[2]

So often we find ourselves settling comfortably amid the unruly tangle of our weeds. Not only do we fail to uproot them, but we make allowances for them. Have you ever told yourself, "It's not that bad" or, "I'll deal with it later"? Have you ever shot a quick glance at somebody else's chaotic landscape and concluded that yours is in pretty good shape after all?

I know I have. But the sin we dismiss could prove to be the most disastrous to our forest.

———————————

Troy didn't see disaster coming. Or more accurately, he didn't want to. He thought his small compromises in the company he co-owned with his friend and business partner, Kevin, would go undetected. The receipts for personal expenditures he'd occasionally submit for reimbursement; claiming "I've got a big client meeting" when he wanted a day off; putting extra miles on his work car to visit his mistress whenever he was near her city. . . .

One evening at dinner, after receiving several rapid-fire texts and ignoring a phone call, a clearly nervous Troy told his wife, "Ah, it's So-and-So [naming a longtime client], and he's upset. I'll call him back later." But his wife had seen that it was an unnamed contact, so she knew Troy was lying. Later, she checked his phone and text logs, and that's when everything went up in flames.

Heartbroken, she confronted her husband, who, after first denying it, finally admitted to the affair. Troy went to Kevin about the troubles in his marriage, and as Kevin probed further, he started connecting some dots between Troy's personal life and his work behavior. Troy ultimately confessed that he'd cheated the company, too, of both time and money. Now he was not only fighting for his marriage, but he was on probation with human resources, and his business partner no longer trusted him.

Cumulative deceptions will undo us. I'm talking about those once-in-a-while visits to the dark corners of the web that grow into a hidden addiction, suffocating a person's spirits and laying waste to his or her relationships. Or our persistent judgment of others that subtly shrouds our hearts in so much pride that we become blind to our flaws. These things may seem inconsequential initially, but they speak to deeper matters of the heart—those areas of our forests that are primed for a wildfire. In fact, the writer of Hebrews says it clearly: "If a field bears thorns and thistles, it is useless. The farmer will soon condemn that field and burn it" (6:8 NLT).

A Sacred Survey

I realize this is a lot to take in. But we have to understand: sin is never small. It is our own knotweed, unsuspicious at first but incredibly destructive. Sin is capable of the kind of infestation that can prevent hope from ever surfacing. That's why it's imperative we get serious about sin.

To experience the full redemptive potential God wants to bring forth in your life, it's vital to surrender everything to Him: your hopes and fears, your doubts and unbelief, as well as your sadness and your sin. Clearing the ground makes way for the good growth of God.

As you begin to examine the types of weeds within your forest, remember that Jesus has already disarmed darkness. Through His triumph on the cross, "he made a public spectacle" of the powers that are against you (Colossians 2:15 NIV). So, if you're worried about how widespread or thick your sin is in certain areas, know this: sin loses its power against the mighty fire of God.

Remember this as well: You have not been left to walk alone. God has given the Holy Spirit as the mightiest of advocates to come alongside you, to help you identify your sin and see it as the abhorrence it is, separating you from God's presence. The Holy Spirit also gives you the desire to eliminate weeds from your forest and is integral in helping you remediate the infestation.

So, we ask the Holy Spirit to lead the way in this sacred search as we open our hearts to the transformative power of humility entwined with hope. We plead with the merciful Father not to leave us unchanged but to harness our times of anguish for a powerful purpose. We cry to Jesus, "In my suffering, sanctify me!"

Which Weeds Are in Your Forest?

Within all of us exist different types of weeds. Nearly every forest, however, has a mix of three types: the native variety, the invasive variety, and overgrowth.

Native sin is of our own doing. It sprouts up as the result of our choices—those times we've taken the enemy's bait that promises what only God can deliver. This type of weed has been rooted in our forests since Adam and Eve's disobedience. They sought to be all-knowing, but many other forms of native sin exist, such as chasing after money to find security, seeking validation in sex, yearning for affirmation through appearance, and striving for purpose through achievements.

For as long as I can remember, my intense desire for acceptance dictated my life. Though at first that may seem like a harmless thing, just look at what that desire bred in me: a tendency to lie if I thought a negative perception was possible. An avoidance of conversation if I feared confrontation. And an ability to abandon my own standards, values, and faith at the drop of a hat. I spent years bowing at the altar of acceptance. And that's only the surface layer of my junk pile.

The Bible clearly teaches that sin is much more than a mere mistake or a minor offense. It's a rebellion against God and a rejection of His authority. Anytime sin is permitted to grow with abandon, we become numb to not only its weight and our desperate need for redemption, but also to God's love—the only power that can save us.

When native sin is pervasive, the transformative power of Jesus's sacrifice on the cross will escape us. Thinking back to the years when I was living for myself, engrossed in ambition and pleasure, I distinctly remember how completely unmoved I was by the gospel. I would hear preachers talk of Jesus's sacrifice, and it was like a small stone hitting an iron wall. I wanted to feel something. I used to feel something.

In time, I started questioning. *Maybe this is proof it just isn't true.* Not until years later, when in desperation I repented and surrendered everything to God, did my heart begin to soften once again. I now often find myself weeping at the mere thought of what Jesus did for me. But for that part of me to be restored, my sin had to be dealt with first.

Invasive sin originates beyond the borders of your forest. It propagates and changes the landscape of your existence wherever the sins of others are introduced into your ecosystem.

All our forests are susceptible to this variety of sin. If you've lived long enough to stand on your own, you've experienced the effects of someone else's sin: mistreatment, addiction, slander, discrimination, betrayal. Unfortunately, if you're in an environment where these behaviors are somewhat normalized, then their effects, like slow-growing vines, can be harder to spot. Without realizing it, an act of injustice buries deep, causing your heart to harden, or a selfish decision seeds resentment that grows undetected, until you're blind to your own bitterness.

I remember sitting on the green leather sectional in our family room. This couch was big. It needed to be to fill the expanse of the great-room addition in our house. This may sound silly, but for twelve-year-old me, that couch was a status symbol. A tangible testament that life was good. So, it's ironic that this is where I was sitting when the bomb went off. My memory from that day is blurred. As if that metaphorical bomb were a literal explosive, fragments of recollection are all I can scrape together.

The words, "We're separating."

My view through the tall windows of our living room as my dad carried boxes to his car.

My tears pitter-pattering on the emerald leather.

Deep sadness, piercing anger, and confusion shaken inside of me, creating a cruel cocktail of grief.

When divorce was introduced into my life, distrust immediately sprouted in my forest. It grew with abandon throughout my adolescence and into my young adulthood. I was always looking for who or what was about to hurt me. I built fences. I tried to self-protect and self-medicate. Some seasons I got a pretty good hold on it; other times, when the conditions were just right, it would grow so fast that it killed off good things inside of me.

Maybe for you, invasive sin grew from words spoken to you that have never lost their power, or from experiencing how someone's disappointment mutated into depression. Invasive sin has an incredible ability to infiltrate.

Whether deliberate or unintentional, this species of sin infests our lives uninvited. We might even turn a blind eye to these intrusions; after all, they're not of our own making. But the hard truth remains: regardless of their origin, the effects of others' sin have taken root in our forests, and they're almost certainly producing offshoots.

For more than half of all adults, trauma has proven to be their forest's most invasive species.[3] Taking the insidious forms of abandonment, betrayal, or abuse, trauma can not only emotionally cripple but also easily seed other sinful decisions. If left to grow, this weed will even choke out good relationships and spread to the forests of those we love.

Trauma burrows so deep that it can exist unnoticed yet influence the way we perceive ourselves and others. Digging up its roots can be painful—especially when other unexpected emotions are unearthed. Somehow, we feel safer keeping things buried.

For that reason, the heat of suffering becomes transformational. In the pain of the flames, you and I often don't have the capacity to continue to bury our pain. In the heat we're more willing to surrender our past. God wants to release us from trauma's unjust grip and burn away what's holding us back. Freedom can be found in the flames.

Finally, **overgrowth** can be a deceptively attractive type of weed. It sprouts when pursuits that may not be inherently bad are left untended. These pursuits often become idols—anything we love more than we love God—and they gradually distance us from Him.

It's ironic, isn't it? We side-eye the Israelites for forging a golden calf to worship shortly after watching God miraculously part the Red Sea, yet we refuse to control our hours after receiving the blessing of a new job. We witness God's generosity in our finances and then struggle to be generous ourselves. We answer His call to ministry and then allow our work for God to take precedence over our relationship with Him.

In her book *Sacred Rhythms*, Ruth Haley Barton beautifully points out:

> Your desire for more of God than you have right now, your longing for love, your need for deeper levels of spiritual transformation than you have experienced so far, is the truest thing about you. You might think that your woundedness or your sinfulness is the truest thing about you or that your giftedness or your personality type or your job title or your identity as husband or wife, mother or father, somehow defines you. But in reality, it is

your desire for God and your capacity to reach for more of God than you have right now that is the deepest essence of who you are.[4]

Overgrowth prevents our deepest essence from coming to life. It blinds us to what really matters in life. Given time, it chokes out our true desire.

Do you know what happens to a grapevine if you don't prune it? It grows and grows with astonishing speed, producing a ton of foliage. Too much. The vine becomes impenetrably dense, blocking out the sun. The grapes suffer. They don't ripen properly, and the plant itself becomes susceptible to diseases, pests, and other problems because of poor air circulation and light penetration. Unless a grapevine is cut back regularly, you'll get puny grapes, fewer of them, and, potentially, the death of the plant.

Cutting back is healthy and can be hard. The good news is, we have a Vinedresser, and His name is Jesus.

Our Saving Grace

This all feels heavy, I know. We've just shone the light on a world of darkness. But the good news is here! We've defined darkness, and now we can look to the One who has defied it.

God knew we didn't have it in us—the ability to reconcile with Him, the strength to defeat the serpent. He could've called it all a loss. After the hundredth time of watching humans spark their own wildfires from the weeds of their lives, you could understand if the love was lost. But it never is. God has made promises to His people. He shows steadfast faithfulness in response to rejection. He stays. Despite it all, God stayed.

And He made a way.

The determined love of the Father that we explored in chapter 2 now comes into physical being. "God so loved the world that he gave his one and only Son, that whoever believes in him shall not perish but have eternal life" (John 3:16 NIV). In an astonishing act of sacrifice to remediate the weeds of sin, God sent His perfect Son to earth. The Father's deepest joy and most profound connection was birthed by a virgin in a lowly stable. The Almighty Himself—wrapped in human flesh that could tear, with human eyes that wept, and with a human heart that felt the weight of every emotion—came to us. The very One who stood alongside the Father during the dawn of creation now found Himself engulfed in the chaotic forest of human existence. The God who crowned His creation with ones made in His image now saves His creation with the One powerful enough to do it: His Son, Jesus Christ.

The Alpha and Omega could have planned a fly-by-night mission with an airplane full of fire retardant. In and out, fire suppressed. No one would be the wiser. But He didn't. He allowed His Son to live among us. To feel our fears, to laugh at our jokes, to grow in real friendship, to attend our celebrations, and to endure rejection. God the Father allowed Jesus to be tempted, to be angry, to be ridiculed, to be betrayed, and to be sentenced to death.

I believe God allowed it so that when the penetrating crown of thorns was forced onto His Son's head . . . when His ripped body was hung on the cross . . . when the blood flowed from His side and He gasped for breath . . . Jesus Christ could, with full understanding, take upon Himself every sin, every injustice, every trouble, and every infirmity.

With a piercing stare that understood it all, Jesus looked death in the face and determinedly declared, "It is finished" (John 19:30). He loosed the chokehold of sin for us with the same intimacy He told the woman at the well everything she had done, with the same deliverance that freed Mary Magdalene from a life bound by sin, with the same power by which He raised Lazarus from the dead, and with the same tenderness with which He took Peter's hand in the storm. Jesus declared us one with Him, once and for all. "Greater love has no one than this, that someone lay down his life for his friends" (John 15:13).

In the quiet expanse of just three days, the depths of human suffering were suddenly illuminated by the most extraordinary news: He's alive! Everything Jesus said is *true*. Now seated at the right hand of the Father in heaven, Jesus Christ awaits the predestined moment when He will return to earth, restoring Eden's fading embers and extinguishing the tormenting flames of pain once and for all.

Donald Barnhouse was pastor of Philadelphia's Tenth Presbyterian Church in the early twentieth century. When cancer took his wife, his daughter was still a young child. One day, when he and his daughter were out driving, they paused at a traffic light, the warm sun shining rays into their car. A large moving truck pulled up beside them, casting a shadow that momentarily darkened the inside of their car. In that moment, Barnhouse turned to his daughter and posed a question: "Would you rather be hit by the shadow or by the truck?"

His daughter quickly replied, "By the shadow, of course. That can't hurt us at all."

Dr. Barnhouse responded, "Did you know that two thousand years ago, the real truck of death hit the Lord Jesus in order that your mother only had to go through the shadow of it?"[5]

Jesus paid it all. He now invites us to turn and follow Him.

A Routine Return

Growing up as a Christian, I found that the word *repentance* always made me squirm. I associated it with the street preacher's shouts of "Repent, lest ye perish!" The word felt heavy, burdensome, and obligating.

Jesus tells us His yoke is easy and His burden is light (Matthew 11:30). He also talks a lot about repentance. So, either Jesus is contradicting Himself, or I had the wrong idea about repentance.

The most common root word for *repentance* in the Hebrew Bible means "to turn" or "to return." Repentance, then, is a call to return to the very heart of God, reclaiming His design for your forest. It's the ability to perpetually adjust your bearings to align with the One whose unwavering desire rests solely on your flourishing.

Is there sometimes a need for a pronounced altar-call confession? Absolutely. However, the beautiful picture of repentance unfolds through the gentle art of routinely turning back, a humble act of restoration. Think of it as a consistent course correction, like a loyal friend nudging you toward the right path. Like fellow adventurers guiding you along an unexplored trail, their gentle "This way" encouraging your every step.

Repentance is an intimate rhythm of return. It beckons you and me to relinquish the illusions that have led us astray, into the weeds, and turn our gaze back to Jesus, knowing we will be forgiven. This is the good news of 1 John 1:8–9: "If we say we have no sin, we deceive ourselves, and the truth is not in us. If we confess our sins, [God] is faithful and just to forgive us our sins and to cleanse us from all unrighteousness."

Do we even realize the matchless gift this is? We don't have to strive. We don't have to earn anything. We can put down our pruning shears and simply follow Him. This is amazing grace, life abundant! This is the freedom to walk in a reality that reconciles our human and heavenly natures. This should make us shout for joy, not squirm with guilt.

The Nature of the Forest

Friends, our forests are both beautiful and bound, growing and gasping, sacred and susceptible. God is aware of our paradoxical nature. He is also the only One who knows the true magnificence of our forest design as it was intended. I can only imagine His profound desire to return us there.

And He will.

For now, let's intentionally carve out time to be with our Creator—a walk in the quiet of the day through our own landscape. Watch as He tenderly points out what's growing. Listen to the cadence of His heart and permit Him to empathize with your struggles. As pastor and prayer warrior Andrew Murray stated, "It is because of the hasty and superficial conversation with God that the sense of sin is so weak and that no motives have power to help you to hate and flee from sin as you should."[6]

God hates sin so much because He loves us so deeply. Remember: the remedy of repentance is simply a return to His heart. That return will purify the air of the smoke that blinds us, helping us see everything more clearly.

IMAGINE: What weeds are growing in your forest? Perhaps some varieties have managed to go unnoticed until this very moment, or maybe you can't escape a persistent nuisance that has tested your resolve for years. Where in your life are weeds blocking out needed sunlight? Where are they choking out abundant life? God is eager to defeat them, but first we must invite Him to help us detect them. Echo the very cry of David: "Search me, God, and know my heart; test me and know my anxious thoughts. See if there is any offensive way in me, and lead me in the way everlasting" (Psalm 139:23–24 NIV). Or pray the Passion Translation of these two verses: "God, I invite your searching gaze into my heart. Examine me through and through; find out everything that may be hidden within me. Put me to the test and sift through all my anxious cares. See if there is any path of pain I'm walking on, and lead me back to your glorious, everlasting way—the path that brings me back to you" (TPT).

4

WHEN THE FIRE SPARKS

My heart skipped a beat when I saw the two lines on the pregnancy test. I squeezed my eyes, wrinkling my nose as I took in the reality of our good fortune. Our son, Max, was newly two, and this pregnancy fit perfectly within our life plan.

Neither Cole nor I admitted it, but as soon as we celebrated the news, we both secretly crossed our fingers for a baby girl to complete our family. For the past fifteen years, I'd been a news anchor, and I had just celebrated my sixth year at a station in Indianapolis. It was my dream job in our dream city. Life felt shiny and bright.

Three other women at the station had recently announced pregnancies, so the creative team came up with a cute (albeit cheesy) announcement video that showed me drinking from a water fountain. As I finish my sip, a coworker leaning against the wall walks away, revealing a sign. "Beware! There's something in the water."

Cheesy. I warned you. But in the realm of local news, viewers become like extended family. They laugh at the silly stunts, follow the daily developments, and truly grow to care about their news teams. So as soon as the video hit the airwaves, we were inundated with well wishes.

Not long after (a couple of weeks maybe), I got hit with a bad cold that made its way to my lungs. Bronchitis, I figured. I was trying to avoid medication, but after my third coughing attack on air, I relented and stopped in at my OB's office on my way to work. The nurse practitioner confirmed my self-diagnosis, prescribed a Z-Pak, and asked if, before I left, I wanted to sneak in to see the baby. Of course!

It was just me and the tech in the ultrasound room. The screens are big these days—it's like watching a movie, except better. I smiled, seeing the little life on the big screen. I already couldn't wait to surprise my husband with the pictures. I was obliviously happy.

That must be why I missed the red flags. In hindsight, they were there. The tech printed off a picture and left the room. She came back, printed off some more, and left again, muttering something about the machine not working. *Take your time*, I thought. *I've got a great view.*

The next time, however, it wasn't the tech who came into the room. It was my nurse practitioner. She walked to my bedside, put a gentle hand on my arm, and said, "Your baby's skull isn't developing. I'm so sorry."

Hot tears clouded my vision as I watched her walk out. By the time the door clicked shut, they were spilling down my face. Confusion like a cloud enveloped me. *What does this mean?* I desperately thought. Then I heard it, a loud whisper to my heart.

"*Emmanuel.*"

"*Emmanuel.*"

"*Emmanuel.*"

My tears stopped momentarily, as if they were listening too. "Emmanuel?" I took in the word that, in my confusion, I could only connect with Christmas (see Matthew 1:23 KJV). My doctor walked in, disrupting the divine delivery.

"It is what we thought," he tenderly said. "Anencephaly. Zero percent chance of survival."

Even now, I remember the scene so vividly. It's just me and the ultrasound tech in the room. She's picking up a few of her things as I put my shoes back on. I'm trying to see through my tears to tie my laces. I know there is one question I need to ask her, but I can barely think, let alone speak. I take the next minute to muster up every ounce of strength I have left inside me, and then I push out the only three words I can manage: "Could . . . you tell?"

She understands, and with a look of sadness so deep I feel I might drown, she says, "It's a girl."

Set Ablaze

I'm sure you remember yours—the spark, the moment you realized your forest was in trouble. For some people, it's gradual, the lingering scent of smoke you tried to ignore. Others are obliviously taking in life's scenery, only to turn and be faced with an inferno that seemingly ignited out of nowhere. Was it a diagnosis for you? A death? A defeated dream? Bankruptcy?

For one online storytelling platform, a filmmaker set up a camera in a makeshift studio on LA's Skid Row and invited those experiencing homelessness and other forms of marginalization to tell their stories.

I'll admit, it was the erratic behavior and the shocking details of life on the streets that kept me glued at first. *Walking cautionary tales*, I thought. But the more I watched, the more I was drawn to these souls—the people beneath the risqué clothes and face tattoos. Their stories, as different as the tapestry of humanity itself, converged on a singular quest: an escape from pain. Yet ironically, every day, they've been subjected to more of it due to addiction and other choices.

The more stories I viewed, the more I realized what was behind my intrigue. It wasn't for the spectacle of their spirals. It was to find *the spark*. In each of their stories, there's always a spark—a trial endured, a trauma survived—that has morphed into a raging wildfire of dangerous behaviors and despair.

Edward's fire started from an unexpected divorce after twenty-seven years of marriage.

Miranda was struck by the lightning of sexual abuse as a young child.

Cindy Lou's fire was started by marital abuse that smoldered for twenty-three years before finally unleashing mayhem.

Michael Molthan's story could've easily ended on Skid Row, or worse. His childhood, marked by sexual abuse, produced a gaping void within him. Attempts to numb the pain turned him to drugs and alcohol, and before he knew it, he had racked up twenty-seven mug shots in four years. The last one brought him to Bradshaw State Jail in Henderson, Texas. The pain he was running from led him to a cell where he was confined for twenty-two hours a day, surrounded by murderers serving life sentences.

In the middle of his despair, he found a Bible that another inmate had been using as a pillow. His curious and illiterate cellmate asked Michael to read to him. He turned to the story of Joseph, a poignant picture of surrendering to God amid pain, abuse, and the confines of a prison cell. He kept reading and eventually learned about Jesus. who can set all captives free.

One night Michael suddenly awoke, convinced he was having a heart attack. He grabbed his chest and exhaled. Feelings of hate, anger, and resentment poured out from within him. Then, inhaling deeply, Michael said he felt ice water flooding his body. An overwhelming surge of love enveloped him. After that night, other inmates began to ask him what he was reading, and Michael started reading the Bible to this group of hopeless criminals. Remarkably, seeds of transformation sprouted. These men began serving and supporting each other. The guards were amazed.

Just two years into his sentence, a paperwork error led to Michael's unexpected release. Unsure of his next steps, he felt God tell him to "walk." He walked three hundred miles back to face the judge to turn himself in on other charges. She told him she had heard what he'd been doing for the other inmates and that she was setting him free. Michael responded, "I'm already free." He was granted a pardon with a promise to pay it forward.

"All the times I was hitting rock bottom, I was always digging to get out of the bottom. . . . This last time I stayed at the bottom. I finally realized that the rock at the bottom at all these times was God. Why would I want to run from the rock? So I stayed next to the rock."[1]

The Fork in Our Forest

The elemental force of fire often sits at a crossroads, ready to chart one of two paths. It can grow out of control, or it can be harnessed by its potential—a powerful crucible capable of the most profound and beautiful transformation available to us humans.

Of that place on our path, author and pastor Dane Ortlund has written, "When life hurts, we immediately find ourselves at an internal fork in the road. Either we take the road of cynicism, withdrawing from openheartedness with God and others, retreating into the felt safety of holding back our desires and longings, lest they hurt again, or we press into greater depth with God than we have ever known."[2]

This is the relational and emotional crossroads that the fires of life bring us to. But there's a crossroads of belief as well. "Either we smirk at what we said we believed about God's sovereignty and goodness, thinking that pain has just disproven what we said we believed," explains Ortlund, "or we put even more weight on our theology. The two circles of professed theology and heart theology, to that point distinct, are forced either to move farther away than ever or to perfectly overlap."

He concludes with our ultimate choice: "Either we let the divine physician continue the operation, or we insist on being wheeled out of the operating room. But pain does not let us go on as before."[3]

Our Obsession with Protection

Oh, how much wiser we would be if we embraced the understanding that pain will not let us go on as before! Yet our culture, cluttered with countless examples, shows people frantically trying to hose down the breaking flames of adversity. We are so threatened by the notion of pain that we've foolishly convinced ourselves we can stave it off or diminish its impact. We try to numb the disheartening news by self-medicating. In the face of inconvenience or hardship, we terminate. We split when relationships become strenuous.

We want life to be carefree and painless, and our decisions often reflect this. Yet in truth, we're not protecting ourselves from anything at all. All the so-called easy decisions still come with incredible grief, but now deep-seated remorse gets to comingle with it, creating a tangled web of regret.

US statistics paint a sobering picture about how we try to avoid pain. As just one example, consider how Americans consume a bewildering 80 percent of the world's global opioid supply.

Please hear me: this isn't condemnation; it's simply an acknowledgment of our relentless pursuit of comfort. This pursuit will slowly drag us into a distorted realm where hardship is hidden and suffering is silenced, no matter the cost. But *we cannot be forged in the fire if we keep jumping out.* We will only walk around with painful burns that remind us of the time we were hurt.

We must, in surrender, stay and hold fast to the only One who can control the flames.

Our Decision to Stay

"We're keeping the baby." Cole's voice was resolute.

He had rushed to the doctor's office as soon as he could. We agreed to meet on another floor, where we would discuss next steps. The nurses graciously offered me a private stairwell so I could descend, literally and emotionally, out of the public's eye.

Cole and I were ushered into a meeting room with a different doctor, whose demeanor was sympathetic but also conditioned toward this type of news. I hadn't been given any details about our daughter's diagnosis, but I assumed the grave conveyance meant she would die very soon in utero, which would require some kind of procedure. Consequently, my first question to the doctor was "What happens next?"

"We don't do it here," she said softly but matter-of-factly. "But you can go to Planned Parenthood."

Planned Parenthood? For a miscarriage?

My cloud of confusion only lifted with Cole's words. *We're keeping the baby.* Abortion hadn't even crossed my mind, and the fact that we were in a Catholic hospital made the suggestion even more surreal.

It wasn't until we got home and did our own research that Cole and I realized our daughter would likely survive full term and that we might even have some time with her. I also read that around 85 percent of anencephaly pregnancies are terminated. This offered context for the doctor's assumption, but no comfort. I thought of all the parents who have faced the same decision. I imagined what it would be like to receive the news at a facility that offers termination right then and there. I wondered how many had made a decision amid the same confusion that overwhelmed me. I wondered why parents aren't first made aware of the potential for life rather than the assumption of death. And I cried again, this time not for myself.

Hide or Seek

Oswald Chambers, who wrote the devotional classic *My Utmost for His Highest*, pointedly observed, "Most of us collapse at the first grip of pain. We sit down at the door of God's purpose and enter a slow death through self-pity. And all the so-called Christian sympathy of others helps us to our deathbed. But God will not. He comes with the grip of the pierced hand of His Son, as if to say, 'Enter into fellowship with Me; arise and shine.'"

Chambers recognized our sufferings as an entrance to intimacy. "Why shouldn't we experience heartbreak?" he wrote. "Through those doorways God is opening up ways of fellowship with His Son."[4]

We will talk more in the chapters ahead about the variety of ways our Creator sovereignly releases hope and opens our hearts to Him through our controlled burns. First, though, we must decide what our response will be: stay or hide. To hide from the pain may always be our inclination—our desire from the shadows of Eden's paradise lost. But to accept God's invitation and seek out intimacy with Jesus will be our saving grace.

At the spark of suffering, friends, remember this: in that pivotal moment, the power to choose is within your hands. No matter how strong or feeble your faith has been to this point, the options are the same. You can smother, numb, or succumb to the pain, or you can surrender it to a God who is intimately acquainted with every depth of despair. May your decision be drenched in courage and bathed in grace, because the consequences—they couldn't be more significant.

IMAGINE: How did your fire ignite? Was it a sudden lightning strike catching you off guard? A discarded cigarette that you just didn't notice? Was it sticks of stress that rubbed together too long? Or a deliberate act of arson? How have you chosen to respond?

Our first instinct can be to frantically grasp for control, wielding our metaphorical buckets of water, desperate to douse the flames ourselves. Conversely, it's also natural to seek escape while attempting to ignore the suffocating smoke. But there's a better way: to face the flames bravely, acknowledging our brokenness yet confident in our position beside the One who directs the winds.

FACING THE FLAMES

Whoosh! The wind blows, strengthening the inferno that's engulfing your personal forest. In the hazy veil of smoke, you strain your eyes, desperately seeking a glimpse of hope amid the relentless flames. Instead, the blaze grows more powerful, conquering the last standing pine tree. Your heart pounds within your chest, trying its best to make sense of the commanding emotions all competing to overtake each other. Anger climbs over sadness, and fear hurries past confusion. As pain pierces the numbness, an anguished plea escapes your lips. A solitary word, forged from the depths of your soul, as if attempting to unravel the disaster before you: "No!" It echoes through the charred expanse, mingling with the crackling of embers.

Questions, heavy with the weight of uncertainty, make their way to the forefront of your mind. *How can this be? Why? What is happening?*

These questions raced through Jon Heckman's mind, clouding his ability to think straight. He was in the middle of designing an anniversary gift for his wife. A gift made from wood—the material symbolic of five years of marriage, representing strength, growth, and a solidified bond. It was an apt token for this milestone in their journey together. After a rocky start, he and his wife had worked hard to reach a place of strength and growth, and their two-year-old son, Jackson, was their walking solidified bond.

As Jon reached for a tool, a distinct thought forced its way to the front of his mind. *Check the house's security cameras.* He didn't know why. He never had before. But he had been away that weekend. As he scrolled through the footage, he realized the cameras had been turned off. All except one. His heart began pounding inside his chest as he watched his wife lead another man to their bedroom.

Jon closed his computer and wept, his wooden gift now reduced to kindling for the inferno in front of him.

He went outside and sat beneath a pine tree. He had always known of Jesus, but he didn't *know* Him. But here, completely broken and alone, Jon looked up to heaven. Tears began streaming down his face, and in a remarkable response, the skies above him opened and began to rain. *He's crying with me.* Jon was somehow certain of it.

Why We Must Go to Gethsemane

In my mind's eye, I picture Jesus leading His disciples on a solemn walk toward the Garden of Gethsemane. The weight of His words from their last supper together—the somber revelation of His impending fate—is lingering in the air, clouding Peter, James, and John in a haze of confusion. They walk in silence, their individual uncertainties consuming them.

As they draw nearer to the garden, I imagine the profound dread that begins to weigh upon Jesus, heavier with every footstep. His pounding heart beats stronger with every minute closer to His nearing betrayal. Jesus instructs His disciples to "sit here" while He goes to pray. And in a raw display of humanity, the Bible tells us, "he began to be sorrowful and troubled" (Matthew 26:37).

Jesus breaks down.

He had been strong the entire night. He had said what needed to be said, but here, with His friends, His composure shatters in raw emotion. The burden He had carried throughout the day, His unwavering strength and resolve, gives way.

I can't help but wonder if any of you have ever had to talk with your loved ones about the limited time you have left on this earth, or if you've been on the receiving end of such devastating news.

I don't know why, but I always imagined Jesus's foretelling of things to be like a camp counselor reading off the schedule for the day—emotionless, obligatory. But oh, the incredible grief of that tender announcement. Jesus had borne the weight of His explanations, fulfilling His duty to communicate clearly. And yet . . . here, in the solitude of the garden, surrounded by three of His dearest friends, Jesus reaches His breaking point. I envision Him pouring out His anguish through gasps of weeping and confessing, "My soul is crushed with grief to the point of death" (v. 38 NLT). I see Peter's head buried in Jesus's neck in a tight embrace; the brothers James and John kneeling beside their friend, their own hearts troubled by His immense sorrow.

Do you dare to imagine yourself there? Kneeling beside this man, clutching His cloak, your tears mixing with His in the dirt, the rhythmic writhing of heartache shared? The release of unguarded sadness? If you've read this far, you almost certainly *are* there already, in your own Gethsemane. Maybe dear friends or family are with you, but maybe not.

Something happens here in this garden, this sacred space. Jesus summons us by name to empathize with His pain even as He promises to empathize with ours. He gently calls us to confront the depths of our own emotions, to offer our hearts and tears as humble offerings in communion with His suffering.

In this vulnerable union we find comfort, yes, but also unbelievable certainty. Certainty that can only come from proximity. Certainty that we are not alone in our pain and that there is only One who holds the power to redeem it. As Charles Spurgeon said, "Infinite power shall stoop that you may lean upon its shoulder."[1]

"I'm Coming with You"

Her kicks would take my breath away and make me laugh, especially when they happened on live TV. Then I would usually choke back tears. Our little girl was not only developing perfectly on schedule, but she was also incredibly active.

We named her Emma Noelle, after her namesake, *Emmanuel*—the name I had heard whispered in the ultrasound room. Even in the confusion that clouded those first few days, my husband and I strongly believed that God had a message to deliver through our baby. We just didn't realize how much that message was directed at us.

Cole and I had taken different paths in our faith journeys. He'd been following Jesus for a few years by this point, and he had always questioned if he was truly saved. I, on the other hand, who'd been a Christian most of my life, always had this sneaking suspicion I was missing something. Although we were involved in church and we each experienced some emotional connection with God on Sundays, the relationship we individually had with God resembled more of a roller coaster than a steady walk. Recurring sin was often lurking, and a persistent, albeit unspoken, question lingered in our hearts: *Is this it?*

After returning home from the doctor's office, our faces swollen and stained with tears, Cole and I sat on the couch and, through sobs, prayed one prayer—just three words: "God, be glorified."

Looking back, I realize our prayer was so simple because we didn't have the strength or the language for anything else. It was a prayer of desperation. It was our gasping in the Garden of Gethsemane. I believe it was in this crossroads moment that Cole and I, feeling totally broken and unworthy, fell to our knees with Jesus and whispered, "We're coming with You."

The Path

There is a route through the old city of Jerusalem named *Via Dolorosa*, which means "Way of Suffering" or "Way of Grief." It is believed to be the path that Jesus walked on the way to His crucifixion.

By the time the wooden cross on which He would die was heaved upon His shoulders, Jesus would've been hard to recognize. In a humiliating spectacle, He'd been sentenced at the Antonia Fortress, where a bloodthirsty crowd demanded a notorious criminal be set free instead of the faultless Christ. A rigged judgment ensued, sealing Jesus's fate with a decree of crucifixion.

Before the brutality of the cross, merciless soldiers orchestrated a staged mockery, stripping Jesus of His clothing and replacing what He wore with a scarlet robe. After twisting together a crown of thorns, they drove the spikes into His skull. Instead of a king's scepter, a reed was thrust into Jesus's right hand, symbolizing false sovereignty. The soldiers' cruelty knew no bounds as they spat on Him, beat Him, and mocked Him with chants of "Hail, King of the Jews!"

If you've ever witnessed someone subjected to relentless bullying, the victim's spirit crushed with humiliation, then let me assure you, what transpired here in Matthew 27 surpassed the depths of cruelty. And this was just the beginning. Bloodied Jesus, in His own clothes once more, forced to His knees with the heavy cross mounted upon His back, was led forward to the Via Dolorosa.

At this time, a passerby was coming in from his field, the Bible tells us (Mark 15:21). He wasn't part of the crowd screaming, "Crucify him!" He wasn't even looking on from the outside. This man, Simon, was doing what he likely did every day: working. The Bible doesn't say if Simon had heard of this Jesus, but we can assume he had heard rumors at least.

The Gospels tell us Simon was a father and a foreigner, an African from the city of Cyrene. Northern Africa. We don't know his ethnicity, but based on how he's identified in Scripture, it's no stretch to assume he looked different from the rest of the crowd. I wonder then, is that why? Is that why, on this pivotal day in history, the Roman soldiers grabbed *him*?

Imagine his fury as the soldiers pushed him to his knees in front of the crowd. Picture his indignation at being humiliated for no reason. Imagine when he realized what he was being made to do. Was it when the weight of the cross was dropped on his shoulders? Did it knock the wind out of his lungs? Had he seen this happen before? Did the blood of another covering that cross stain his clothes?

How could he not be grieved by the injustice this day had brought? The thoughts racing through his mind, *Are my sons watching this? Someone make sure they're not.* And then, rising to his feet, I imagine the scene in front of him coming into focus.

A man. *Is that a man?* Nearly dead already. The frame of a human, blood-covered and too weak to even carry his own cross. And in the chaos of the moment, in the middle of the venomous shouts from the crowd, I imagine Jesus, supported by the lowest-ranking soldiers, blood dripping down His face . . . turning.

Simon, halfway to standing under the weight of the wood, pauses. Their eyes lock. Simon's breath catches. The eyes of this man—he knows them. How could he know them? And then he realizes, *No, these eyes know me.*

One second feels like a lifetime, and somehow, this dead man walking is comforting the one carrying His cross. Somehow, all the injustice Simon feels fades in this man's presence. Somehow, Simon knows he's exactly where he needs to be.

In the Fire

I wonder . . . after the climb to Golgotha, after Simon's forced labor was served, after the last of the soldier's incendiary comments was hurled, did he stay? Did Simon continue to fix his gaze on those eyes? Did he squeeze his own eyes shut when the soldiers pounded the nails into Jesus's hands and feet? Did he dare object when the spear pierced the dying man's side? Did Simon wonder who Jesus was talking to when, in His final breath, He declared, "It is finished"? Did he feel the earth quake? See the rocks split? Did he watch the skies darken? Could he hear the loud rip of the temple curtain being torn in two? Did he witness the centurion and all who were with him exclaim, "Truly this was the Son of God!" (Matthew 27:54)? Did he run home to tell his family? Did he stay until all the others left?

We don't know the details, but we do know this: in the middle of the ordinary—having done nothing to deserve it—Simon of Cyrene was cast into one of the darkest hours in history. And it was there, amid the turmoil, that he met Jesus.

Baptism from Fire

This also we know for sure: meeting Jesus changed Simon forever.

How do we know? There is only one account of this man in the Gospels. It is one sentence long. If you're like me, you've overlooked it many times. But don't dismiss it this time. There's an intriguing and specific reason it's included in the Scriptures. That sentence states, "And they compelled a passerby, Simon of Cyrene, who was coming in from the country, the father of Alexander and Rufus, to carry his cross" (Mark 15:21).

You know. Simon. The father of Alexander and Rufus.

Mark, the author of this specific account, was writing to his readers as though they knew of this family, as though this family were part of the early church. Not only that, but a segment within church tradition believes Simon went on to become an evangelist and a martyr.

It's worth a moment to ponder: Was it Simon's suffering that brought him into relationship with Jesus? Did Simon's suffering bring *his sons* into relationship with Jesus? You see, other people were there that day: the crowds, the mourners. But because of Simon's *suffering*, he was likely closer to Jesus than anyone.

Can you imagine with me Simon the Cyrene sitting at a table with friends and fellow believers years after the resurrection? "Simon, tell us again. What did He say? Simon! What did you see? How did He look at you? Tell us, what did you feel?"

Can you imagine the other Simon, named Peter? The man who loved Jesus fiercely yet denied knowing Him three times just hours before the walk to Calvary? Can you imagine how much he wished he could've been the one to carry the cross?

I told you earlier about Jon Heckman, who inadvertently discovered his wife's infidelity caught on video. Jon's suffering brought him to the feet of Jesus too. Through the pain of his separation and eventual divorce, Jon made a conscious decision to surrender everything to Jesus. He was baptized and willfully chose to pick up his own cross and follow in the footsteps of his Savior. Balancing the responsibilities of a single working father, Jon also served and led at his church, all while raising his son in the ways of the Lord.

It had been six years since Jon's fire erupted when I reached out to him about sharing his story. His journey hasn't neatly been tied up with a pretty bow of reconciliation or even a new love. He's still carrying his cross, and I wondered what his response to my personal request might be.

Jon's reply was immediate and unwavering: "My posture is that the story is the Lord's. Use it however the Spirit leads!"

Next came these words: "I'll loop back. I'm out right now and baptizing my son in the morning."

Was it Jon's suffering that led him into relationship with Jesus? Was it Jon's suffering that led *his son* into relationship with Jesus?

Absolutely.

From Simon of Cyrene to Jon of Indianapolis, God never changes. His faithfulness never fails. His goodness knows no bounds to those who are willing to pick up their cross and follow Jesus.

Throughout history, this truth has not changed, lessened, wavered, or been found errant. More than one hundred years ago, in 1915—a year marked by incredible challenges that included a world war, major political reforms, racial segregation, and women's suffrage—a Pentecostal journal titled *The Transforming Power of Suffering* was published. It said in part:

Through suffering, we gain a deeper revelation of the redemptive work of Jesus Christ. As we bear the weight of affliction, we identify with His sacrificial love, His compassion for the broken and hurting, and His victory over sin and death. Suffering teaches us the fragility of our earthly

existence, humbling us to acknowledge our dependence on God's sustaining grace and power. In our
weakness, His strength is made perfect. . . . May
we find solace in the truth that our Savior walks
with us in our darkest hours, and as we surrender
our pain and anguish to Him, He turns our suffering into a catalyst for His divine purpose.[2]

Because of the suddenness of suffering, it often seems
random. Simon didn't have time to prepare, and I'm
willing to guess you didn't either. No one asked Simon if
he thought it was fair. I'm guessing that no one asked you
if you were busy with something else. In suffering, we are
simply called to pick up our cross, lock eyes with Jesus,
and follow Him down the Via Dolorosa.

The Perspective of Pain

Just days before Simon the Cyrene's sacred encounter with
Jesus, a profound dialogue unfolded between Christ and
His disciples. Although it wasn't an explicit reference to
that instance, Jesus imparted a crucial teaching, declaring
that *every* person must shoulder his or her own cross
to follow Him. In fact, this remarkable statement was
made right after Jesus's memorable words to Peter, "Get

behind me, Satan!" (Matthew 16:23). You remember that exchange. The one when Jesus rebuked Peter for his failure to prioritize heavenly matters.

In the next breath, Jesus turned to His disciples and declared, "If anyone would come after me, let him deny himself and take up his cross and follow me. For whoever would save his life will lose it, but whoever loses his life for my sake will find it" (vv. 24–25).

Simon found his life in Christ by picking up the cross. And Jesus is telling us that we can too.

The gospel of Jesus Christ is immeasurably powerful for those who believe. Jesus's life, His sacrificial death, and His triumphant ascension provide unending revelation of who God is and what He has done, is doing, and will do through the fire. Yet somehow, we as believers are prone to limit its scope. "Yeah, I get it. The gospel. Jesus died for my sins."

But if we stop there, at a ticket to heaven, we're missing something major. We're missing the faith confession, the pivotal moment when we can say, "I no longer live, but Christ lives in me" . . . and *mean it*. It's a critical choice, a massive leap of faith. But here's our incredible opportunity: it's *here*, in the flames of adversity, where our hearts expand to rightly perceive His love, where our eyes open to new revelations of His abundance, and where our hunger for divine truth grows. This union with Christ and His cross produces something altogether distinct, beautiful, and astonishingly powerful *in us*.

Amid your blazing inferno, when thoughts of survival and self-preservation want to consume every ounce of your being, allow yourself to lock eyes with Jesus on your own Via Dolorosa. Gain your strength from His example and trust that, just like Simon, and just like Jon Heckman, and just like me . . . He's at work in *your* pain, more than you can fathom.

IMAGINE: Your eyes burn from the billowing smoke. The crack of a giant pine toppled by the flames startles you. The fire is growing, but you realize you're not alone; Jesus is right beside you.

A deer bounds from a thicket in front of you, desperate to escape. You can't believe the injustice of it all. You are certain you don't have what it takes to survive this. You turn, almost forgetting Jesus is there. Your eyes lock on His gaze. With a sound more like rushing water than actual words, Jesus simply says, "I know." And somehow, someway, you know you can trust Him.

Every one of us wants an encounter like that. If you've never dared envision yourself weeping with

Jesus or carrying His cross, I encourage you to go there. To let down any guard of self-protection or inhibition and ask Him to meet you where you are. He's better and more beautiful than you or I can possibly imagine.

REFINING FIRE

The men were trapped, and they knew it. Lying face down in the dirt, all they could do was listen. They never imagined fire could sound this way. Hell had unleashed its wrath upon an astonishing three million acres of land in the northwestern United States, and Ed Pulaski and his team of firefighters had done everything they could to save the town of Wallace, Idaho. At the last minute, on Pulaski's orders, the crew escaped to an abandoned mine tunnel, thinking this was likely the end for them.

It was the summer of 1910. A wildfire of unprecedented proportions was etching its name in history as the "Great Fire of 1910" or the "Big Blowup." This catastrophic event was sparked by a sequence of lightning strikes. Fueled by dry conditions and strong winds, the fire quickly grew out of control. Entire forests were devoured, ancient trees decimated. Ultimately, the blaze burned everything in an area roughly the size of Connecticut. Journals from that time recount towering columns of smoke and flames, painting an apocalyptic scene that terrified residents and firefighters alike.

The firefighters, having only rudimentary resources and strategies, were immensely outmatched by the blaze that raged uncontrollably for several weeks. The fledgling US Forest Service and local volunteers fought tirelessly alongside them, but no one was equipped to combat such an enormous fire.

That summer day, Pulaski—a ranger with the US Forest Service—and his crew of forty-five firefighters found themselves at the forefront of the blaze. They worked tirelessly to protect the small Idaho town as flames raced toward the community. Panicked residents evacuated by train as Pulaski's men fought the encroaching wall of fire.

While working on one section of land just outside the town, a new surge of fire erupted out of control, overwhelming the crew. Pulaski realized his team would not be able to outrun the fire, so he led them into an abandoned mine tunnel before venturing back out to assess the situation.

As Pulaski surveyed the area, he saw that the fire had cut off their escape route, leaving them trapped. Knowing immediate action was needed to survive, he hatched a daring plan: Pulaski instructed his crew to use their shovels and dig a trench, removing any flammable material and creating a bare patch of ground around the entrance of the tunnel. With flames licking at the edge of the clearing, Pulaski realized another problem: mere shovels wouldn't be enough to create a firebreak. So, he fashioned a new tool from a combination of an ax and a hoe. Several of Pulaski's men followed suit, and they all worked feverishly, using this tool to dig a wider trench, battling flames and embers as they went. The fire raged closer, throwing scalding heat and smoke. The men fought on, their determination unwavering.

Finally, just as the flames reached the clearing, Pulaski ordered his crew back into the tunnel, faces down. The firestorm raged overhead, but the bare ground around the tunnel entrance held the gap against the advancing inferno. Inside the tunnel, the firefighters anxiously awaited their fate. Time crawled by as the roar of the flames echoed through the darkness, but eventually, the sounds subsided. The crew emerged from the tunnel to a scene of devastation but with their lives and most of the town of Wallace spared.

Ed Pulaski's innovative tactics and his creation of the Pulaski tool not only saved lives but left an indelible mark on firefighting techniques. His invention continues to be widely used by firefighters to this day.

The Great Fire of 1910 would claim the lives of eighty-seven people, including both valiant firefighters and innocent civilians. The loss of human life was compounded by the destruction of countless homes, infrastructure, and livestock, causing immeasurable economic and emotional devastation.

There's no denying the ruthless toll taken by the fires of life. The ache of loss hurts deeply, perhaps unbearably. Even burns that are controlled can't guarantee a return to normal or regrowth resembling what once flourished. But like Ed Pulaski, we can seize unexpected possibilities from even the most threatening circumstances to allow for revelation and rescue.

When Pain Meets Purpose

I cautiously step into this chapter with a keen awareness that assigning "purpose" to suffering can seem harsh or insensitive. Depending on where you are in your journey, this notion of purposeful pain can carry with it a profound hope or a visceral contempt. If the latter is true of you, I understand. I've been there. However, my prayer is that as we explore the profound ways God uses our pain, we'll find greater healing and deeper hope.

We've all witnessed the effects of uncontrolled pain—whether something as common as an ugly divorce or as paramount as genocide. These are the wildfires of life. Devoid of any purpose beyond devastation, wildfires engulf everything in their path without restraint or reason. Their rampage knows no bounds, damaging landscapes for generations.

By contrast, a controlled burn represents an entirely different essence—one of purpose, promise, and boundaries. Redemption arises within the realm of a controlled burn. A chance to revitalize the landscape and nurture new growth from the ashes of the old. A controlled burn embraces the wisdom of restraint and thoughtful direction, offering the opportunity to channel destruction into renewal.

God knows how to do just that. Scripture reminds us He is the source of all that is good and perfect. Because this is true, a fascinating paradox emerges from pain: *God can use it for a mighty purpose if we give Him the opportunity.* We see this paradox in Genesis 50:20: "As for you, you meant evil against me, but God meant it for good."

But before we get to the goodness—the redemption—before we even explore the promise and boundaries of a controlled burn, let's address the question that inevitably arises from any fire: *Why does a good God allow bad things to happen?*

Five Purposes of Fire

Scholars and theologians have written entire books on this subject, but one thing I want you to hear from *this* book is that God never desires our suffering, and He certainly doesn't delight in it, no matter how transformative it might be. The God of Justice (*Yahweh-Tsidkenu*) despises suffering even more than we do.

Simply put, suffering is the result of sin—this shattered state that arose when humanity chose self-interest over submission to God. As we've seen, pain was never intended as part of God's grand design. What *was* intended as part of His design is free will—that remarkable capacity given to us to shape our own destinies. For God to eliminate suffering, He would have to erase our free will, reducing humans to spiritless robots. Instead, He longs for a genuine relationship with us, flawed and messy as we are.

Doesn't it make sense? This relentless wrestling with the *why* of suffering stems from an innate awareness that suffering is not inherent to our creation. Deep within our souls, we yearn to be restored to God's original design. Listen to what Paul says in Romans 8:22–23: "We know that all creation has been groaning as in the pains of childbirth right up to the present time. And we believers also groan, even though we have the Holy Spirit within us as a foretaste of future glory, *for we long for our bodies to be released from sin and suffering.* We, too, wait with eager hope for the day when God will give us our full rights as his adopted children, including the new bodies he has promised us" (NLT, emphasis mine).

That word *groaning* drags my own memories to the surface. I think of times after Cole and I learned of our baby's prognosis when I crumbled onto my closet floor, the carpet absorbing my tears. Moments when I had no words to spare, no prayer to pray, no strength to stand. Just groaning— guttural grief expressing more than any verbal plea.

Paul knew about this kind of anguish firsthand. What we read in Romans 8 isn't some pie-in-the-sky language from someone who's oblivious to suffering. He speaks not only of longing but also of groaning and waiting for the day of promise. No one's implying here that we ignore or deny the weight of pain. Paul isn't advising us to look past suffering. Instead, he's instructing us to gaze through it. To cradle both healing and hope delicately, letting each strengthen the other.

With this in mind, let's briefly venture into some of the main purposes of the fiery crucible of suffering.

1. Sharing in Christ's Sufferings

As deeply as we delved into the concept of sharing in Christ's suffering in the previous chapter, we just scratched the surface of scriptural truth on this topic. But allow me one more powerful account, that of the apostle Paul, who wrote to the Philippians while he was imprisoned. His words in this letter were meant to encourage them to stand firm in their faith and live in a manner worthy of the gospel of Christ. Paul expresses the extraordinary value he places on knowing Christ Jesus as his Lord. He considers everything else as insignificant compared to this surpassing worth. Paul willingly endured the loss of all things, considering them as worthless, so he could gain Christ and be found in Him. The righteousness the apostle sought didn't come from adhering to the law but rather through faith in Christ, so that he could "know him and the power of his resurrection, and . . . share his sufferings, becoming like him in his death" (Philippians 3:10).

As the saying goes, "To know him is to love him." When we actively participate in Christ's suffering, the profound truth of the gospel moves beyond mere intellectual understanding and takes root deep within our hearts. This intimate connection with Christ is the ultimate outcome of our next purpose: determining if our faith is real.

2. Testing and Refining Faith

One of the most pivotal purposes of pain is the testing of our faith. In the flames of adversity, our faith undergoes a rigorous examination. Here, trust in God is either forged and strengthened or unmasked as a mere pretense. Here, genuine faith is separated from superficial belief.

You see, a dangerous condition afflicts those who have only an intellectual belief in God. Without the transformative essence of the gospel of Jesus Christ having permeated their hearts (often a direct effect of suffering), biblical knowledge and spiritual tradition turn stale in the mind. And with no vital lifeblood from the heart, the gospel remains cold at best. This is also when the gospel is most likely to be weaponized against others to fan the flames of *their* fires. Westboro Baptist Church in Topeka, Kansas, comes to mind—a group of people who identify with Christianity yet promote immense hatred, division, and bigotry. While this is an extreme case, similar dynamics happen on a small scale to many people. I call it a "gospel blockage," when a person intellectually aligns with the teachings of Jesus, but Christ's grace and truth have not reached his or her heart.

There is perhaps no greater cure for this gospel blockage than pain. Pain is what typically brings us to the exam room (or the emergency room) for diagnosis, and then—often—straight to surgery. On the spiritual operating table, the foundations of faith are scrutinized, its authenticity laid bare. God takes the pain in His expert hands and, from it, creates an antidote for hardened hearts. Paradoxically, pain is many times exactly what's needed to dislodge the blockages and allow for an infusion of gospel vitality.

Using a different metaphor, Peter reminds us, "These trials will show that your faith is genuine. It is being tested as fire tests and purifies gold—though your faith is far more precious than mere gold. So when your faith remains strong through many trials, it will bring you much praise and glory and honor on the day when Jesus Christ is revealed to the whole world" (1 Peter 1:7 NLT).

He's saying that the hotter the flame, the more impurities can be extracted. That's the process with gold. There is only one way gold is purified, and it's not over the gentle flicker of a candle. Gold must be plunged into the center of a roaring fire. It must endure the excruciating blue heat—the kind that makes the days of the mild orange flame seem not so bad. Only by staying in that searing intensity can gold shed its impurities, lose its resemblance to its former condition, and be shaped to the goldsmith's intent.

The same is true for us. In the scalding heat of tribulation, our self-righteousness can float to the top, our doubt can be discarded, and our pride can be strained away.

If our pain doesn't refine us, God knows it will define us. Why else would He allow His chosen people, the Israelites, to suffer through forty years of wilderness wandering before delivering them to the Promised Land? Based on the distance of their journey and the number of people involved, it might have taken weeks to cross the desert, but forty years? God freed them from slavery in Egypt, only for the Israelites to refuse to appreciate and adhere to the boundaries He'd lovingly set for them. They let the remnants of their pain erupt into a wildfire of suffering. They fanned the flames with false gods, grumbling, and immorality.

Imagine with me a journal entry from an Israelite after the thirty-seventh year of wilderness wandering. Maybe it would sound something like this:

The barren landscape seems to extend endlessly. In this harsh wilderness, the scorching heat of day is matched only by the piercing cold of night. Supplies are scarce. I complained to Moses, again. Oh, how I miss the variety of food we had in Egypt. The availability of water. Living in a home, no matter how humble, rather than a tent. The smells of the market.

The Promised Land feels far away. They talk of this land flowing with milk and honey, a land of freedom and abundance. But I don't know how much longer I can hold out hope. . . .

Pastor Charles Spurgeon delivered a sermon in 1889 in which he addressed the wanderings of the Israelites: "Israel gained by education," he said. "The Lord was not going to lead a mob of slaves into Canaan, to go and behave like slaves there. They had to be tutored. The wilderness was the Oxford and Cambridge for God's students. There they went to the University, and he taught and trained them, and they took their degree before they entered into the promised land. There is no University for a Christian like that of sorrow and trial."[1]

You and I are also awaiting a promised land. It's coming. But no one will force us to go to class. We can spend our time on earth skipping class, complaining about the workload, and copying others' papers, or we can see our time on earth for what it really is: a profound allotment we've been given. A free (to us) education bought and paid for by the blood of Jesus. A time to learn, grow, and receive revelation that will prepare us for what's coming.

Now, imagine the same person's journal entry three years later:

Today is a day I will never forget—the culmination of generations of hopes and dreams. We have finally entered the long-awaited Promised Land, a gift from Yahweh Himself. The moment we set foot in this land, a surge of emotions overwhelmed me. It is more beautiful than any description could capture. I wish Moses could see this. As I gaze upon the abundance, I can't help but reflect on the long and difficult journey that brought us here. The wilderness is where we shed the mindset of slavery and embraced our identity as a chosen people. It is the place that taught us humility, trust, and dependence on the Almighty.

There were moments when the Promised Land seemed like an unattainable dream, and I questioned whether it was worth the struggles. But standing here, I am now more confident than ever, not in myself, but in the God who led us out of Egypt. The same God who fulfilled His promise to us.

We don't know what lies ahead, but we know who will continue to lead us. I'm reminded of the Lord's words to Joshua: "Be strong and courageous. Do not be afraid; do not be discouraged, for the Lord your God will be with you wherever you go."

This land is new. This chapter is new. And I am, in so many ways, new.

3. Attaining Spiritual Growth and Maturity

Have you ever met someone who seems to have a flawless life without any real difficulties? Be cautious of quick judgments; most of us bear far more than we readily reveal. Yet if I were to encounter someone who truly leads a life without struggles, I'd be willing to bet that they're actually marked by immaturity. They might find it difficult to express compassion and empathy. Perhaps they give up on things that don't come easily. I expect that they tend to rely more on their own abilities than on God's provision. True maturity, whether spiritual or in any other aspect of life, is usually cultivated through hardship. In suffering, we learn valuable lessons and develop resilience. (Incidentally, this is why we shouldn't shield our children from all hardships either.)

I also want to emphasize this crucial point: maturity should not be mistaken for perfection. It's all too easy to confuse the two, but let me assure you, they are not the same. The road toward maturity is often a wild and messy ride, riddled with missteps, moments of false humility, and even failure. We must let go of the idea of attaining perfection and instead embrace the reality that we all mess up from time to time.

In fact, recognizing and acknowledging our imperfections is a significant indicator of spiritual growth. We are called to receive salvation *and* to grow in our relationship with Christ. As Paul said in Ephesians 4:15, "We are to grow up in every way into him who is the head, into Christ." This implies an ongoing process of learning and aligning ourselves with Jesus.

James wrote, "Consider it pure joy, my brothers and sisters, whenever you face trials of many kinds, because you know that the testing of your faith produces perseverance. Let perseverance finish its work so that you may be mature and complete, not lacking anything" (James 1:2–4 NIV). He advises us not to view suffering as an obstacle blocking God's plans or evidence of its failure, but to recognize pain's powerful role in shaping our maturity. In the darkness our roots can grow deep enough to survive any storm. The rich soil of experience nurtures our reliance on God, cultivates empathy and compassion for others, and fosters a profound understanding of an eternal perspective. In this fertile ground, our maturity takes root.

Addressing the immense potential for growth amid trial, author Paul David Tripp has written:

> Rather than being signs of God's inattention, [moments of difficulty] are sure signs of the zeal of his redemptive love. In grace, he leads you where you didn't plan to go in order to produce in you what you couldn't achieve on your own. In these moments, he works to alter the values of your heart so that you let go of your little kingdom of one and give yourself to his kingdom of glory and grace. God is working right now, but not so much to give us predictable, comfortable and pleasurable lives. He isn't so much working to transform our circumstances as he is working through hard circumstances to transform you and me. Perhaps in hard moments, when we are tempted to wonder where God's grace is, it is grace that we are getting, but not grace in the

form of a soft pillow or a cool drink. Rather, in those moments, we are being blessed with the heart-transforming grace of difficulty because the God who loves us knows that this is exactly the grace we need.[2]

4. Accepting God's Discipline and Correction

Although much of the pain we encounter results from living in a broken world, some trials we face are the direct outcomes of our own decisions and actions. In these moments, we must view God's discipline and correction for what they are: acts of love, mercy, and grace. Whether His guidance comes in the form of gentle nudges toward growth or the fierce fire of refinement, God is always acting on our behalf, providing us precisely with what we need. In Psalm 119:75–76 (NLT), we gain insight into the psalmist's understanding of God's discipline: "I know, O LORD, that your regulations are fair; you disciplined me because I needed it. Now let your unfailing love comfort me, just as you promised me, your servant."

God's discipline is not a flagrant reaction. He isn't sitting in heaven doling out punishments that match the offense. Rather, in love, God's correction is carefully tailored to redirect our paths and bring us closer to Him.

Like a caring parent who knows the most effective way to discipline his or her child, God possesses an intimate knowledge of each one of us. Thus, He can shape us in ways that capture our attention, prompting us to turn back toward Him and encouraging us to flourish in His love. Hebrews 12:6–7 reminds us that just as a loving parent disciplines a child out of care and concern, God does the same. His correction is never condemning but eternally rooted in an unwavering love—a love that longs to see us become who we were created to be, image bearers of God Himself.

In 1779, John Newton wrote a hymn that aptly describes the purposes of godly discipline:

> I asked the Lord that I might grow
> In faith and love and ev'ry grace,
> Might more of His salvation know,
> And seek more earnestly His face.
>
> 'Twas He who taught me thus to pray,
> And He, I trust, has answered prayer,
> But it has been in such a way
> As almost drove me to despair.
>
> I hoped that in some favored hour
> At once He'd answer my request
> And, by His love's constraining pow'r,
> Subdue my sins and give me rest.

Instead of this, He made me feel
The hidden evils of my heart
And let the angry pow'rs of hell
Assault my soul in ev'ry part.

Yea, more with His own hand He seemed
Intent to aggravate my woe,
Crossed all the fair designs I schemed,
Humbled my heart and laid me low.

"Lord, why is this," I trembling cried;
"Wilt Thou pursue Thy worm to death?"
"'Tis in this way," the Lord replied,
"I answer prayer for grace and faith."

"These inward trials I employ
From self and pride to set thee free
And break thy schemes of earthly joy
That thou may'st find thy all in Me."[3]

5. Pursuing God's Glory and Honor

Ultimately, for those who walk the path of Christ, their suffering brings glory to God. While enduring a prolonged period of testing, the apostle Paul recounted in 2 Corinthians 12 how he pleaded with the Lord to take away his burden. God's response was this: "My grace is sufficient for you, for my power is made perfect in weakness" (v. 9).

When we persist through trials, trusting in God's faithfulness, our lives become a living testament to His power. Our suffering becomes a platform for God to display His boundless grace, mercy, and love. As others witness our unwavering faith, they are irresistibly drawn to the God who sustains us.

At the same time, we are pushed to fervently pray. God sometimes reveals His glory and power through divine interventions and miracles, and sometimes we witness it in the simple faithfulness of people who stay true to Him. Through those who steadfastly hope in Him and grow stronger in their hope, even as the fire gets hotter.

Cole and I had clung to this purpose of glorifying God since the day of Emma's diagnosis. But we also knew the inferno was far from over. Our hope was in God; we just prayed that as the flames intensified, we would not fail *Him*.

Twenty-One Sacred Minutes

For six months, I anchored the nightly news while my belly continued to grow. Although some days were incredibly hard, something greater than myself sustained me, and I knew it. I would anchor a newscast, return to my desk, and try to respond to some of the hundreds of emails and letters that arrived daily, and then do it again the next day. I had something many parents of infant loss don't—acknowledgment and support—because we had shared our story with so many, including my viewers. This outward support helped me cope with the reality that was never far from my consciousness: we would soon be saying hello and goodbye to our daughter.

The days were long, but somehow the months slipped through my grasp. And just like that, the day of delivery stood before us, an unwavering guard standing at the threshold to the unknown. With Cole's hand clutching mine, we walked under the covered entrance of the women's hospital and through the revolving doors, our spirits strengthened by the collective pleas of countless prayer warriors. The soft light of that early morning in March transitioned to fluorescents overhead as I was wheeled into the operating room. A team of doctors and nurses quietly prepared for my scheduled C-section, the event I had imagined for months with such anticipation and trepidation. But as I looked around the room, a peculiar peace settled over me that blanketed my anxious heart. I was ready.

It was in that hallowed space that Emma was born alive. The nurse lovingly handed her to Cole first. I remember the lines etched on his brow, a deep furrow as he looked into his daughter's eyes. I wondered what he was feeling. In the middle of my contemplation, the anesthesiologist asked how I was feeling. At the sound of my response, Emma turned her gaze toward me, recognizing her mama's voice.

With fatherly tenderness, Cole placed our daughter in my arms, a weightless miracle cradled against the heart she'd heard beating for eight months. She was small, her tiny pink hat perched just above her eyes, hiding the truth of the condition that would soon claim her life. I stared at her, drinking in the sight of her tender face, her sweet lips. In a hushed whisper I told her things I had longed to say.

"I love you, Emma."

"Do you know how many people love you?"

"I'm so proud of you."

And finally, with bittersweet surrender, I uttered the words of release: "You can go, sweet girl."

I handed her back to Cole, and it was there, twenty-one sacred minutes later, that she passed from her daddy's arms into her heavenly Father's. The nurse took her pulse, and with a soft nod, let us know she was gone.

The enemy of our souls yearns for us to disregard eternity as nothing more than wishful thinking, a fairy tale to be dismissed. But for Emma and every cherished child of God who has passed from this life, heaven is more real than any fleeting moment this earthly existence offers. This glorious actuality awaits our weary souls on the other side of suffering.

C. S. Lewis penned these profound words in a letter: "We ought to give thanks for all fortune: if it is good, because it is good, if bad, because it works in us patience, humility and the contempt of this world and the hope of our eternal country."[4]

Heaven is coming. Pain is preparing us. That's not just a purpose . . . that's one powerful promise.

IMAGINE: Fire possesses the remarkable ability to both cleanse and consume, to mold and to mutate. Its transformative power refuses to let anything remain unchanged. As you continue to walk through your controlled burn, gently consider what changes are stirring within you. Have certain longings been extinguished, or have new ones ignited? Has a new understanding given you sturdier footing for the rest of the journey? The blistering flames of suffering demand transformation. We can walk around forever scarred, or we can be intentionally shaped.

THE TRANSFORMATIVE WASTELAND

Through squinted eyes, you look around, bewildered. "Where am I?" you mutter, your voice tinged with desperation. The once-commanding presence of the tall evergreen trees, whose towering forms used to point you toward the river in your forest, have vanished. A hauntingly desolate scene unfolds before you. Ashes swirl with the wind, a choreographed dance of confusion and despair.

You climb to the once-breathtaking vista, only to see an apocalyptic valley of smoke and charred wood. The field that used to be your sanctuary—a haven of wild grasses and shady oaks—now lies before you as a barren wasteland. In this surreal moment, pangs of loss sound in your soul. Everything you've nurtured and tended throughout the years, every precious seed you carefully sowed, seems lost. Unspeakable grief washes over you.

This is the valley of death: death of a loved one, death of a relationship, death of a dream, death of security. It's dark here. This place can consume a soul with fear and anguish. Hope can feel a million miles away. The promise of suffering is yet to be revealed. But here, the gift of Emmanuel is made tangible. Nothing is required of you other than to trust that He is with you. "Even though I walk through the valley of the shadow of death, I will fear no evil, for you are with me" (Psalm 23:4). Here, in the ashes of the wasteland, our conviction that He is enough becomes irrefutable.

At this juncture in our journey with Emma, on many days I didn't even have the strength to pray. I could only wake up and put one foot in front of the other. I experienced why the wasteland is so transformative: it confronts us with our limitations and vulnerabilities, leaving us nothing else to hide behind. At the same time, that feeling of utter vulnerability is unsettling. The fire has exposed what lies beneath—things we need to process and consider.

At this point, most of us want to pack up whatever we have left, abandoning these acres of scorched earth and the truth of what has happened. We find the reality too sad, too hard, too costly. But the fire has exposed an opportunity that wasn't possible before. Not at this level. An opportunity to further prepare the ashy ground for the new growth that is already underway. An opportunity to make determined decisions to allow ourselves to feel . . . and to forgive.

Determined to Feel

This is what our society has unwittingly taught us . . .

Wipe that soot off your brow and put on a happy face.
If anyone asks, claim you're "doing OK." That's an honest
   enough response.
If a surge of emotion threatens to surface, shove it right
   back down where it belongs. You've got this!
Chronic illness? Downplay the pain.
A relationship teetering on the edge? Don't even mention it.
Clouded by the shadows of depression? Force a smile.

It's not that we purposefully strive for inauthenticity; we're simply scared of feeling sad ourselves or causing others to feel uncomfortable by our pain. Still, "there's no such thing as selective emotional numbing," according to renowned researcher and author Brené Brown. "There is a full spectrum of human emotions and when we numb the dark, we numb the light."[1]

Here in the West, we thread our "pursuit of happiness" throughout the fabric of our culture. We are recognized worldwide for this combination of hope and ambition.

The downside? Over time, our desire for "happiness above all else" diminishes our ability to rightfully express or even recognize sadness. Culture has so conditioned many of us to recoil at the touch of negative emotions that we no longer give ourselves permission to feel them. Think about it: If a person appears unhappy in public, would you be concerned? How many times has someone apologized to you for getting choked up? How many times have you apologized for the same? Yet research indicates that experiencing and accepting emotions like anger and sadness is crucial for processing and healing from grief.

Sadness serves many purposes, including helping us remember what we desire and cherish. Sadness facilitates personal reflection after a loss, enabling us to come to terms with life's harsh realities. And for Christians, this process invites us into the ring with God Himself, where He wants us to hurl our honest emotions and questions at Him.

Deflecting Disappointment

As it turns out, the real emotion most of us tend to avoid is disappointment, a close relative of sadness. I wonder if we avoid addressing our disappointments because we're scared of where they might lead. Lost faith? Hopelessness? Bitterness?

God can handle our disappointment. He invites us to bring it to Him so He can minister to our hearts and give us closure and healing.

While we're in the ring with Him, here's an ironic punch in the gut: the more we try to avoid these emotions, the more hopeless we feel.

In 1987, Daniel Wegner conducted a thought trial known as the white bear experiment. The experiment involved two different groups of people. The first group was instructed to speak freely for five minutes while trying not to think about a white bear. Each time the bear came to mind, they were to ring a bell. Next, the same group was instructed to do the same exercise, but this time while thinking about a white bear.

A second group of participants was instructed from the get-go to think about a white bear as they conversed and to ring a bell each time the bear came to mind.

Researchers discovered that the group who had initially suppressed their thoughts of the bear, though later given the freedom to do otherwise, rang the bell far more frequently than the group who had not been initially told to suppress their thoughts.[2]

This shows that attempts to suppress certain thoughts can bring them to mind even more. So, if we avoid expressing sadness, we might unwittingly think about our pain more, which would affect us at deeper levels.

At some point I realized that for most of my life I had avoided sadness. Since negative feelings were my kryptonite, I was an expert at pushing them down and moving on. I remember standing in church many Sundays after Emma's death. Certain songs would evoke such deep sadness that all I wanted to do was curl up on the floor and sob. Instead, I choked back the tears and counted the minutes until I could race out to the car, where I could truly allow myself to unravel. Rather than letting others share in my grief, I chose to carry the burden alone until it would get too heavy, and then I'd lash out at Cole with the ridiculous accusation "You're not sad enough!" After that, I would pick up my grief once more and trudge along alone.

Oh, what we're missing by our lack of lament! The ability to come alongside each other in truth and vulnerability; the opportunity for our brothers and sisters in Christ to minister to us; the power of the Holy Spirit that comes upon God's people when together they call on His name in times of trouble. . . . In the church, we almost exclusively sing of victory and strength while failing to recognize that one in every three psalms are laments. Cries of anguish: "How long, O LORD? Will you forget me forever?" (13:1a). "Out of the depths I cry to you, O LORD!" (130:1). "How long will you hide your face from me?" (13:1b).

Our culture's loss of lament, this pressure to project a put-together image, has created a fake and weak version of Christianity. The false face won't let us be real, when being real is an important element of a controlled burn. If there's no place for sorrow in the church—if you and I believe that, even here, we cannot let down and talk of how we truly feel—we will always project a level of inauthenticity. What's more, if we're not revealing the extent of our weakness to each other, we are inadvertently magnifying our power, not God's. Because His power is only made perfect in our weakness (2 Corinthians 12:9).

To be clear, the psalmists didn't lament to simply express their emotions or to make room for endless weeping. They conveyed the raw reality of their circumstances while standing on a truth even more apparent after the fire had cleared the surface of their forests: ultimately, they had victory. Their psalms proclaimed that the worse their situation and the hotter their fires, the deeper their trust in God's providence.

The Art of Lament

If anyone stood on scorched earth after a fiery trial, it was the Jewish people in the Old Testament book of Lamentations. This collection of poetic dirges, or laments, mourns the destruction of the city of Jerusalem and the Jewish temple by the Babylonians in 586 BCE. The book is believed to have been written by the prophet Jeremiah shortly after the destruction, during a time of profound sorrow and grief. He wrote in raw detail of the loss of the city's splendor, the ruin of the temple, and the people's suffering due to devastating famine, extreme violence, and crushing exile.

Besides the book of Job, Lamentations is probably the most painful and horrific in its descriptions of suffering, with statements such as "My eyes are spent with weeping; my stomach churns; my bile is poured out to the ground because of the destruction of the daughter of my people, because infants and babies faint in the streets of the city" (2:11). Lamentations spills forth the anguish and sorrow felt within the religious fabric of a nation. Remarkably, it simultaneously stands as the most meticulously structured book of the Bible—the first four chapters are acrostics, each verse beginning with a distinct letter from the Hebrew alphabet.

Why would God, in all His wisdom, choose to inspire the most grotesque descriptions of suffering in such a way? One suggestion: Lamentations hints that our pain is not arbitrary. Rather, it's purposeful, contained. God has erected boundaries around our pain. Lamentations 3:31–33 explicitly promises, "The Lord will not cast off forever, but, though he cause grief, he will have compassion according to the abundance of his steadfast love; for he does not afflict from his heart or grieve the children of men."

Within the structure of this book, we find a plan for our pain. A divine arrangement that whispers of goodness yet to come for the children of God. A promise that the abundance of God's heart lies not in affliction but in compassion. He has made a way for His goodness to prevail.

In Lamentations, God uses an art form to communicate that this judgment is not His last word. He promises a new covenant for His beloved people. Ultimately, Lamentations points to the redemptive work of Christ. The book doesn't end in despair but serves as a catalyst for trust and hope.

In his 1897 essay "What Is Art?" Leo Tolstoy acknowledged art's profound ability to communicate emotion. But he took it even further, believing the true purpose of art to be empathy: "Art is a human activity, consisting in this, that one man consciously, by means of certain external signs, hands on to others feelings he has lived through, and that other people are infected by these feelings, and also experience them."[3] We see his point nowhere clearer than on the cross itself.

Did you know that Jesus, in His anguish, recited someone else's poetry? Matthew 27:46 reports, "About the ninth hour Jesus cried out with a loud voice, saying, 'Eli, Eli lema sabachthani?' that is, 'My God, my God, why have you forsaken me?'" This was a direct quote from the beginning of Psalm 22:1, David's poetic cry during a time of despair.

Neither Jesus nor David was alleging that God had abandoned him. Rather, both were expressing deep emotion, united in their grief. In the same way, our own expression of sorrow can help others find solace and understanding. Tolstoy would argue that to withhold this is to do all of humanity a great disservice.

Heaven's Example

Perhaps we can give ourselves more permission to lament when we realize how much heaven cares about our sorrow.

The Bible assures us that God meticulously keeps account of our every tear, collecting them in a bottle and recording each one in His book (Psalm 56:8). All of heaven recognizes that tears were never intended to be part of God's original creation. The angels' hearts must ache at witnessing our grief and watching us navigate through a reality so far removed from the perfect existence we knew before the fall.

At the same time, all of heaven eagerly awaits that glorious day when everything will be made right. When death is no more, and mourning and pain will cease. The day when God presents each of us with our bottle of tears. When He opens His book and we behold His hand amid our heartaches and His unwavering provision in our pain. When we see His goodness amid our grief and His shocking love that comforted us in loss.

Until then, lamenting is how we engage in dialogue with God in the middle of our pain. Through lament, we acknowledge His sovereignty, seek His comfort, and trust in His faithfulness from within the fire and beyond it. Lament provides an avenue for emotional release, allowing us to process grief and find solace in God's presence.

Lamenting in truth births a profound form of praise to our heavenly Father that exceeds any words we can utter in times of abundance. And it sprouts the true hope that has been residing beneath the surface all along.

Consider the transformation that would sweep across the church (and within our own hearts!) if we shed our pride, became vulnerable in our trials, and granted God His rightful place in our laments. Going even further, what would happen if we took seriously Paul's instruction to bear one another's burdens and weep with those who weep? Brené Brown's research and conversations with thousands of people have brought her to a telling admission: "I have started to believe that crying with strangers in person could save the world."[4]

I personally believe we would witness powerful moves of God that, in turn, would fashion kingdom warriors, forged in the fire, who stand unashamed and unrestrained.

Determined to Forgive (Others)

Lament unites believers in shared sorrow, fostering empathy and compassion within the church. It promotes a culture of support where, having received help in our fire, we can in return offer comfort and encouragement to others who mourn, strengthening the bonds of fellowship.

This is what can happen and what should happen. But there's a very real chance that this hasn't been your experience.

Let's go back to the Garden of Gethsemane for a minute. Jesus, His spirit heavy with impending suffering, has just bared His soul to His beloved disciples, His urgent words revealing His imminent arrest. He asks the three men to pray and keep watch. And in a powerful response to Jesus's anguish, they gather around, committing to keep watch all night and diligently pray for their Lord's strength to endure.

Oh wait, no. They fall asleep.

Following Jesus's vulnerable moment with Peter, James, and John, we witness the scene unfold starting with Matthew 26:39:

> Going a little farther [Jesus] fell on his face and prayed, saying, "My Father, if it be possible, let this cup pass from me; nevertheless, not as I will, but as you will." And he came to the disciples and found them sleeping. And he said to Peter, "So, could you not watch with me one hour? Watch and pray that you may not enter into temptation. The spirit indeed is willing, but the flesh is weak." Again, for the second time, he went away and prayed, "My Father, if this cannot pass unless I drink it, your will be done." And again he came and found them sleeping, for their eyes were heavy. So, leaving them again, he went away and prayed for the third time, saying the same words again. Then he came to the disciples and said to them, "Sleep and take

your rest later on. See, the hour is at hand, and the
Son of Man is betrayed into the hands of sinners.
Rise, let us be going; see, my betrayer is at hand."
(vv. 39–46)

Not once, not twice, but three times, the disciples fell
asleep at one of the most pivotal times in friendship—and
in history.

Before we wag our fingers, I want us to connect with
the frailty of the disciples. I don't think their drowsiness
was born out of disinterest or lack of compassion. They
had faithfully followed Jesus through thick and thin. I
think they were exhausted. And as much as each of us
would like to believe we would be the lone alert disciple,
the truth is, we're all flawed and bound by limitations.
And this universal truth holds a difficult implication for
us: in times of suffering, people will inevitably let us down.

Can you not hear the exasperation in Jesus's words to
Peter: "Couldn't you at least keep your eyes open for one
hour!?" Have you, in your moments of pain, ever experienced frustration at the response of others, or the lack
thereof? You anticipated one thing from a person, only
to receive another. You assumed someone would act in
a certain manner, yet he didn't. You relied on someone
to be there, but she was absent. In life, but especially in

times of adversity, people will both surprise and disappoint you.

Countless relationships have fractured in the wake of suffering. It is natural to feel hurt by others, but we must recognize that, even unknowingly, we have been the cause of disappointment too.

There are a thousand reasons why some people don't show up the way you hoped. Maybe they're walking a rough road, unknown to you, or they're paralyzed by their inability to express themselves during trying times. Other people haven't been through a fire yet—or at least not the type of fire you've experienced—and they simply cannot relate. I encourage you, instead of chopping down that tree out of anger or frustration, take it to Jesus. Allow the Holy Spirit to minister to your wounded heart. Be honest with yourself and with God about the pain you feel, and if you feel compelled, communicate to that person that you wish he or she had been there for you, while offering forgiveness wholeheartedly.

Your offender's response might surprise you. It could be a source of guilt for him, a burden she's eager to release. Alternatively, it might signal that it's time for you to find solace and support from other sources. There are others who *will* in fact surprise you with profound and unexpected support.

Regardless of anyone else's response, it's crucial for us to be aware of resentment's tendency to ride shotgun with suffering—and our consequent need to extend grace or mercy, for our own sakes above all.

Paul urged the church in Ephesus regarding this very thing. He told them, "Be angry and do not sin; do not let the sun go down on your anger, and give no opportunity to the devil" (Ephesians 4:26–27). In essence he was saying, "It's understandable that you're hurt. But you have to decide what you do with that. And if you choose to let it fester, the enemy will use it to thwart the redemption, the profound regrowth that God wants to bring to your forest."

Impossible Forgiveness

That's all well and good, you may be thinking, *but someone started my fire. How can I forgive that?*

"To the two teenagers who started the wildfire," the letter started.

Barely a month had passed since the fire consumed Michael Reed's house, claiming the lives of his wife and daughters. Not just fire—arson. A deliberate act orchestrated by two teenagers who were now charged with setting the fire in the Great Smoky Mountains National

Park that ultimately destroyed thousands of homes and killed fourteen people. Constance Reed and her precious daughters, Chloe and Lily, were counted among the victims. Michael, along with his son, stood as the lone survivors of their tight-knit family.

As the harsh reality of Michael's charred landscape sank in, he wrote these words to the very people who had stripped him of everything: "As humans, it is sometimes hard to show grace. We hold grudges. We stay angry. We point the finger and feel we have to lay the blame somewhere. . . . But I did not raise my children to live with hate."

And then, in a profound act of release, Michael Reed said to the boys, "I forgive you. My son forgives you. My wife and beautiful girls forgive you. . . . We will pray for you. Every day. We will pray for your parents and your family members. Every day. We will pray for your peace. We will show you grace. Why? Because that's what Jesus would do."[5]

In fact, it *is* what Jesus did. As He struggled for breath, sweat and blood pouring from His pores, Jesus made a plea on behalf of the very people who were crucifying Him: "Father, forgive them, for they know not what they do" (Luke 23:34). There was no remorse from the savage crowd in return. No reconciliation. Appallingly, the soldiers continued to mock Jesus mercilessly while gambling for His clothing as He hung dying.

Long before His crucifixion, while Jesus was delivering His Sermon on the Mount, He issued one of His most serious warnings. He told His followers, "If you forgive other people when they sin against you, your heavenly Father will also forgive you. But if you do not forgive others their sins, your Father will not forgive your sins" (Matthew 6:14–15 NIV).

Gulp.

For me, and maybe for you, too, it's surprisingly easy to trivialize this directive. *God always forgives, doesn't He? Surely His grace covers me if I can't find it within myself to forgive.* Yet Jesus's words are crystal clear. He holds nothing back. Forgiveness holds serious weight in the kingdom of God. He leads by example, and He wants us to extend the same to those who have wronged us.

How she treated me is unforgivable.

But you don't know what he did.

Here's the truth. Forgiveness, at its core, aligns you with *God* rather than the person you forgive. Forgiveness is birthed from God's heart—because He is holy—and He invites you to share in His divine nature through forgiveness. There's nothing easy about it for our human nature. Every fiber within us is determined to hold the grudge and harbor hatred. But within forgiveness, something supernatural unfolds. You and I shed the calloused layers of our humanity and put on the righteousness of Jesus Christ Himself.

We bring heaven to earth.

One of the reasons we find it so hard to forgive is that we confuse forgiveness with reconciliation. Sometimes the two go hand in hand, but oftentimes not. Forgiveness stands as a deliberate choice, irrespective of the relational outcome. It is an unwarranted pardon of transgression, a relinquishment of our right to anger. And it's *hard*. In fact, forgiveness borders on the impossible unless we first grasp on a profound level the forgiveness given to us.

You see, the forgiveness we receive from God can never be matched. Whatever you are asked to forgive will never come close to the forgiveness you have received. Psalm 103:10–11 (NLT) says, "[The Lord] does not punish us for all our sins; he does not deal harshly with us, as we deserve. For his unfailing love toward those who fear him is as great as the height of the heavens above the earth."

The deeper I internalize that it was *my* sin that nailed Jesus to the cross, the more I fathom the profound pardon offered *me* at Calvary, and the more I am empowered to extend forgiveness to others. Forgiveness is not a chore to carry out. It is an outgrowth of the new creation God is nurturing in us.

We cannot force forgiveness through white-knuckled determination. We cannot simply try to be more forgiving. That may work for a short time, but with the first negative memory or emotion, you and I will get sucked right back into the quicksand of bitterness. We need the freedom that true forgiveness offers us. The freedom that comes from focusing on the extravagant forgiveness we have received from God—and subsequently extending it to others.

Forgiveness is the greatest of gifts paid for at the highest of costs. No matter what happens with that person who wronged you, forgiving makes you right with God. It releases your desire for retribution and ushers you into the fullness of who you are in Christ.

Determined to Forgive (Ourselves)

The three days following Emma's birth and death, Cole and I were blessed to have her with us in our hospital room, thanks to a device called a CuddleCot. It's a cooling bassinet that allows extra time with your baby for bonding and closure. We were able to take pictures, and our families were able to hold her. It was a profound gift of time.

I'll admit, there were many parts of our journey that scared me. I never looked at Emma's head, for instance. I kept it covered by her hat. The second morning after delivery, I gingerly walked to the CuddleCot. I wasn't sure how our baby girl would look forty-eight hours past her death. As I peered in, I was struck by her appearance. She had somehow settled into her features. Her nose was a perfect button, and her lips were the most perfect, doll-like shape. She was stunningly beautiful. I knew I should take a picture. But her lips were a dark purple—the color that made it perfectly clear this was a baby's dead body in the bassinet.

I didn't know how to feel or how to process it.

I didn't take the picture.

I didn't take the picture.

I'd give anything for that picture now, to be able to look again at my daughter's precious face that day. To remember that moment of mortality, that time when *scary* and *sacred* overlapped.

I regret my decision.

Is there perchance anything you regret from your fire? No one prepares us for the flames, so it's understandable that we sometimes make decisions we come to regret.

Maybe it was you who lit the match that set your forest ablaze . . . So maybe the forgiveness you need to extend is to yourself.

Regardless of the extent of your regret, can I suggest something? Will you share it with Jesus? Will you tell Him about the lost opportunities that keep you up at night, and the reminders of that one bad decision that meet you every morning? Regrets kept hidden can easily turn to shame. And they're the last thing your hurting heart needs. Jesus wants to free you from the bondage of regret. In Philippians 3:13–14, Paul wrote, "One thing I do: forgetting what lies behind and straining forward to what lies ahead, I press on toward the goal for the prize of the upward call of God in Christ Jesus."

Just think of Peter's regret after denying his friend and Savior three times before His death. "Peter remembered the saying of Jesus, 'Before the rooster crows, you will deny me three times.' And he went out and wept bitterly" (Matthew 26:75). Peter lamented. He repented.

We are not alone in our suffering.

We are not alone in our grieving.

We are not alone in our forgiving.

Peter could have chosen to wallow in his missteps. He could have listened to Satan's accusations. But he didn't. Peter maintained faith in the finished work of Christ. He would go on to become a prominent leader among the disciples, a powerful preacher to the early church, a radical evangelist, a performer and receiver of miracles, and the author of two books of the Bible.

Resentment and regret are dangerous kin—silent partners that prefer to stay deep within the hidden confines of our hearts. They do their most effective work in the shadows, covertly attaching to our thoughts and convictions, incessantly picking at the scabs of our healing wounds. We must bring them into the light, where we can see their effects clearly, and then stomp them out once and for all.

Take Heart

The searing agony that rages through the scorched earth of suffering will leave you breathless. In these tumultuous moments, hot spots smolder with the possibility of rekindling, threatening to engulf you once more. Your forest feels like hell on earth, and it is. But do not lose heart. A pivotal moment awaits you just around the bend, a time ripe with the promise of revelation. Like the first rays of dawn breaking through the darkest night, you are on the cusp of a profound understanding. Concealed beneath the layers of ash left behind by the controlled burn of your life lies a treasure trove of hidden riches. Although those riches may be obscured by the remnants of your past struggles, they remain perfectly intact, awaiting discovery.

In the face of adversity, we might find ourselves consumed by the desolation and anguish. But we cannot forget the transformative power that lives within each of us. You are created to be a resilient being—not for the purpose of mustering up a façade of strength, but for the goal of embracing the truth that this life can be bigger, more important, and more freeing than any days you've lived prior.

So, take heart, and press on. Allow yourself to feel, to forgive, and to hold fast to the hope that a bountiful harvest awaits.

IMAGINE: Create space in your life for lament, even if simply by spending time with God outdoors—getting some solitude—or connecting with others through a support group like GriefShare, Al-Anon, or DivorceCare, where you have a safe place to open up and process your emotions.

For those of us skilled at keeping a tight rein on our emotions, what type of art might help you express lament? Creative writing? Painting? Composing or listening to music? Dance?

These spaces and forms for expression tend to expose feelings that reside beneath our awareness. Here's why: they require openness.

Art in particular allows us to creatively embrace life in its entirety—the hidden depths, the splendor, the elegance, the chaos, and the raw reality. Art articulates what words alone often fail to communicate. To attempt to navigate suffering without a creative outlet could cause you to miss a major opportunity for healing. Will you give it a chance?

8

INFINITE PROMISES, FINITE BOUNDARIES

I had walked through a diagnosis, pregnancy, delivery, and death, but one day loomed before me that I dreaded most and feared with every fiber of my being. *How could I possibly leave the hospital without my daughter?*

I awoke that third and final morning at the hospital with tears already streaming down my face. Had I been dreaming? How did my body know? Very slowly I turned my head to look over at Emma nestled gently in her bassinet beside my hospital bed. The sight of her petite profile unleashed an unfathomable sorrow that surged from the depths of my soul. I squeezed my eyelids shut in a futile attempt to hold back the dam of despair. Hot tears defiantly poured down my cheeks and neck in rebellion, the cotton of my pale green hospital gown their final resting grounds. As if grief itself had a sound, a guttural groan pushed its way out of my mouth. In utter desperation, I cried out to God, "I can't do this!" I had been through so much. But *this*, leaving her, I was certain would physically break my heart.

It's difficult to put into words, but in that instant when my strength had been stripped away and I was utterly defenseless against the encroaching despair, I felt an extraordinary surge of supernatural strength. A swell of inexplicable power coursed from the bottom of my feet to the top of my head. A profound, palpable peace fell on me that somehow obliterated my fear. There was no doubt in my mind: I had just received the aid of heaven itself, and not even death could stand against its power.

If I had ever thought of Emmanuel as just another name for God, I now knew better. *My God, my Savior, my friend* is *with me*. And in that moment, I realized He is everything I could ever want or need.

Together, Cole and I spent the morning tenderly rocking Emma and saying our final goodbyes. When the time came to leave, we handed her to our nurse, who continued rocking her as we left the hospital room and walked through the revolving doors that had ushered us in three days earlier. Settling into the car, we buckled our seat belts, looked at each other, and . . . smiled. It was the bittersweet smile of gratitude within sorrow. We had just experienced the unimaginable. We had just lived out the decision that some said was crazy. We had just walked through fire, and miraculously we weren't burned.

Please hear me. The grief wasn't suddenly gone, and the searing pain of loss hadn't disappeared. But in that moment, I realized that those things didn't hold the power I had feared they would. Something unlocked within me, a seed of increased faith that had been lying dormant. I felt a profound assurance that what I had said I believed all my life—that God is good, that He never leaves us, that Jesus defeated death—had all proved true to me.

Profound Promises

"Your promise revives me; it comforts me in all my troubles," wrote the psalmist (Psalm 119:50 NLT).

While we might long to understand the purposes of pain, really, we most desperately need God's *promise* when the fires of life are raging. The redeeming quality of a controlled burn lies in the guaranteed positive results it delivers. What is true for the landscape is true for our lives.

The promise of God in our suffering is twofold. First, He promises that the fire is temporary. Second, He promises that the glory of eternity will redeem it all. We see both of these represented in 2 Corinthians 4:17: "For this light momentary affliction is preparing for us an eternal weight of glory beyond all comparison."

Still, I find it strange that Paul chose the word "light" to describe the afflictions the early church was enduring. Persecution by the Roman Empire, martyrdom, internal division and heresy, social ostracism—none of that seems light to me. And I'm sure your pain doesn't feel light either. But Paul was trying to shift the focus, though not like some people do. He was not suggesting, "Oh, your suffering isn't a big deal. Move on." He was not saying, "Get over it." His words offer a perspective that can help our minds heal while our bodies and hearts are recovering.

When my son falls down, bloodying his knee, I don't tell him to look at the blood. I don't tell him to focus on the pain. I show him a Popsicle, and while I'm tending to his wound, his attention turns to what's coming. It doesn't lessen his pain, and I don't tell him he shouldn't feel sad. I try to help him put his situation into perspective, knowing that, one day soon, his scrape isn't going to look or feel like it does right now. I think Paul was doing the same thing, saying, "I know this hurts, but look over here."

So, what is this "eternal glory" that Paul referenced? Right now, on earth, we as believers have access to incredible gifts. But eternal glory is what awaits believers in Christ for eternity.

It's impossible for us to know everything that is ahead. The Bible tells us no eye has seen, no ear has heard, no mind has imagined what God has prepared for those who love him (1 Corinthians 2:9). Still, what we do know is enough to uplift even the most burdened soul. Here's a short list:

- We know we will be in the presence of God Himself, enjoying unhindered fellowship and communion with our Creator.
- We know we will be freed from sin and the struggles of the flesh.
- We know our transformation into the likeness of Christ will be complete. We will thoroughly reflect His character and glory.
- We know we will receive heavenly rewards.
- We know that all of God's promises will be fulfilled.
- And perhaps most stunning of all, we know we will stand in awe at the unveiling of God's majesty. The full revelation of His power and splendor will be ours in a way we can't possibly understand here and now.

Paul acknowledged that right now we can't see things clearly. Right now, our understanding is imperfect, "like puzzling reflections in a mirror." But one day, he reminds us, "we will see everything with perfect clarity. All that I know now is partial and incomplete," he says, "but then I will know everything completely, just as God now knows me completely" (1 Corinthians 13:12 NLT).

On the day of Jesus's return, His church will stand as a spotless bride. And our path to purification will be paved by the refining fires of this life. The pain of those flames will burn away what tethers us to this world and leave us desperate for the living flame of Jesus. *His* fire will consume us, driving out all other affections and distractions, setting us apart. We will become spotless simply by turning and beholding Him.

The eternal weight of glory beyond all comparison is not an empty promise or a mere consolation. It is a powerful reality that the difficulties we endure in this life are temporary when compared to the everlasting glory that awaits us.

Heavenly Help

As we attempt to grasp the immense promises of God, may we be profoundly encouraged to remember the saints who have gone before us, followers of Christ who were intimately acquainted with suffering. Beautiful souls who walked through fire. A great "cloud of witnesses," the Bible calls them, who in this very moment are urging *you* on from heaven (Hebrews 12:1).

I think of Catherine of Alexandria, the daughter of a Roman governor, who embraced the teachings of Jesus Christ. As she passionately spread the gospel message and spoke out against the unjust executions of believers, she caught the attention of the emperor, who sentenced her to death. While Catherine awaited her fate in prison, hundreds of people visited her and were inspired to embrace faith in Jesus.

I think of Horatio Spafford, a successful nineteenth-century lawyer and devout believer. His son died of scarlet fever in 1871, and shortly thereafter, the Great Chicago Fire destroyed most of Spafford's investment properties, putting him in financial difficulty. Just a few years later, he planned a trip to Europe with his family but had to send his wife and daughters ahead of him. Their ship collided with another vessel in the middle of the Atlantic Ocean, killing all four of his daughters. While sailing to meet his grieving wife, his ship passed by the location where his girls had lost their lives. There he penned the famous hymn "It Is Well with My Soul," with words that still resound in churches around the world[1]:

When peace, like a river, attendeth my way,
When sorrows like sea billows roll;
Whatever my lot, Thou hast taught me to say,
It is well, it is well with my soul.[2]

I think of German pastor and staunch anti-Nazi dissident Dietrich Bonhoeffer, who fervently encouraged the church to oppose the profound injustices of the Holocaust. Even while imprisoned, Bonhoeffer remained resolute in his mission. Tragically, mere weeks before the end of World War II, he was executed at the Flossenbürg concentration camp. A small scrap of paper was smuggled out of Bonhoeffer's prison cell just before his death. On it was scratched these words: "Only the suffering God can help."

As you stand at the crossroads of affliction, I imagine these mighty men and women of God summoning the strength of the Savior on your behalf. They're coaxing you to walk the path of tender trust and to fall with abandon into the loving arms of God. They're imploring you to reject despair, bitterness, and defeat. To push against the darkness and reach for the light. I envision them emboldening you with shouts of "He's worth it all!" and "This isn't the end of your story."

On those days when your grief wants to succumb to despair, remind yourself that you are not alone on this path. Throughout the ages, countless saints have walked it before you, and they have borne witness that the hope of Christ is real. That He gives life through the fire. In their stories and their footsteps, you'll find profound evidence that the decision to run to or from God in your pain matters more than you can imagine.

Boundaries in the Blaze

The promised result of a controlled burn is what compels the forest ranger to light the torch. Yet the carefully drawn boundaries within that burn provide the hope for what lies ahead: the promise fulfilled.

Boundaries are the most crucial element to contain a blaze. They are the very things that don't exist in the chaos of a wildfire . . . and they were God's idea.

In the beginning was God—and it took Him just one day to implement boundaries: on day two, He created the sky to separate the waters of the earth from the waters of the heavens; then on day three, God created dry ground to separate the waters on earth. In Jeremiah 5:22, the Lord confirms, "I made the sand a boundary for the sea, an everlasting barrier it cannot cross. The waves may roll, but they cannot prevail; they may roar, but they cannot cross it" (NIV).

Enter humans, and from the start, they are given limits too. Not only regarding the tree of the knowledge of good and evil, as we've seen, but regarding where they will dwell and what they will do there. For example, Genesis 2:15 reveals, "The LORD God took the man and put him in the Garden of Eden to work it and take care of it" (NIV). And in Genesis 1, we read God's command (and blessing!) to the man and woman: "Be fruitful and increase in number; fill the earth and subdue it. Rule over the fish in the sea and the birds in the sky and over every living creature that moves on the ground" (v. 28 NIV).

In this perfect place, boundaries served as an integral part of its perfection—and an integral form of God's blessing.

Our Boundaries

From Genesis we know that boundaries are good.

They're also necessary to contain the flames of life's fires. God knew that if there were no boundaries for the vast oceans, humans would drown. And in a lot of ways, that's exactly what happens when we lack boundaries in suffering: We drown in expectations, regret, and bitterness. We end up disoriented by the smoke, just trying to survive the fire.

No one's boundary lines are the same, however. Just as every prescribed burn requires different parameters, every person traversing trials will need unique boundaries. For Cole and me, the most significant boundary materialized with our first prayer, which became our mission statement: "God, be glorified." That boundary allowed us to discern what stayed in our forest and what stayed out. Additionally, it helped me filter what I shared with the public and why.

I needed that aspect because, during more than a decade as a news anchor, I had become well-versed in sounding and looking put together. In other words, I could fake it with the best of them. But in the wake of the baby's diagnosis, I drew a figurative line in the fire of authenticity. I fought the temptation to present our pain in a way that would make me seem stronger than I was or elicit attention. "God, be glorified" became the sieve. Through it, I could sift out my flawed intentions.

One week after Cole and I received Emma's diagnosis, a friend and photographer from my news station, Shawn, was scheduled to come to our home to take pictures. These photos were meant to accompany a blog I had decided to write about our heart-wrenching news.

Early that morning, on the day of the photo shoot, I awoke with a pressing thought. I shot off a message: "Hey, Shawn, if you see this in time, could you bring a video camera?" The notion that jarred me from my sleep was the realization that writing a blog would allow me to carefully craft my words. I could shape the narrative, softening the hard reality we were facing, or portraying myself as somewhat composed despite being shattered. So, when Shawn arrived, video camera in hand, I asked him to set up a tripod and simply hit Record.

Cole and I hadn't planned a single word of what we were about to say. We simply bared our souls, shedding tears and clinging to the hope somehow rising within us. It was raw, ugly, and undeniably real. As it turned out, that video made its way around the world, initiating a different broadcast for me—one that would last six months and be closely watched by hundreds of thousands of people we would never have had the chance to reach otherwise.

I had chosen authenticity as a boundary mainly to protect my heart from my own wayward tendencies, but it also protected me from others' expectations. It may strike you as strange, but it's true that when someone suffers, people inevitably place expectations on them. Your extended family or friends, your coworkers, even your fellow church members may be expecting you to behave in a certain way or believe for a certain thing. Others may seek to use your story for their benefit. And it's practically guaranteed that countless voices will offer unsolicited advice. But remember

this: your audience must always and only consist of one—
the One who knows your heart intimately.

To accomplish this, you may have to be deliberately intentional with others during this season. Perhaps you limit the voices in the conversation to ones who are in line with God's Word, as a friend of mine did. Or maybe you make known that for a time, you are saying no to invitations, obligations, or volunteering. You may even pause or discontinue certain types of news, social media, or forms of entertainment. Give yourself permission to carry out whatever limits God may be calling you to. If you are not intentional, people will unintentionally trample barriers, inadvertently releasing the contained flames. Sit down with the Lord and pose the question, "What boundaries do I need in this season?" And await the still, small voice that will gently guide you.

God's Boundaries

Let's not forget the most important boundaries of all. Scripture is clear that God Himself draws boundaries around us in our suffering. Perhaps nowhere is that more evident than in the story of Job.

A righteous and prosperous man, Job found himself subjected to unimaginable trials and tribulations due to a celestial dialogue between God and Satan. The Bible informs us that God called Satan's attention to Job, proudly proclaiming his righteousness and devotion. Satan challenged God's assertion, arguing that Job's piety was solely based on his wealth and his comfortable life. If God were to remove these blessings, contended Satan, Job would abandon his faith.

Curiously, God accepted Satan's challenge and allowed him to afflict Job, but there is a divine caveat: God set limits on the extent to which Job could be tested. God establishes a boundary, a line beyond which Satan cannot go. This showcases God's unwavering sovereignty over the situations of all our lives. The Lord ensured that Job's suffering had a purpose and would not break him beyond repair.

As the biblical narrative progresses, horrific events unfold for Job with relentless intensity. He loses his wealth as his livestock is stolen. His servants are killed. Then a devastating storm demolishes his son's house, killing all his children. Despite these heart-wrenching trials, Job remains steadfast in his faith, "The LORD gave, and the LORD has taken away; blessed be the name of the LORD" (Job 1:21). That was Job's boundary line: *I will trust God's sovereignty even though I don't understand the reasons for this suffering*. We are hearing his faith boundary inside the lines God had sovereignly drawn, which Job could not see.

INFINITE PROMISES, FINITE BOUNDARIES

Satan, not content with the initial results, is granted permission by God to afflict Job physically, but is again bound by the Almighty's limitations. Job is struck with painful boils from head to toe, reducing him to a pitiful state. His wife tells him to curse God and die. Despite his immense suffering, Job refuses.

Job's statements and actions aren't coming from someone denying their fire or their feelings. Not only did Job sit in sackcloth and ashes as expressions of the depth of his grief, but for most of the book of Job's forty-two chapters, he wrestles with his questions and his understanding of God.

How does Job's story end? With a celebration of his strength and sheer grit? With a deconstructed faith? No. His story ends with a transforming realization of God's infinite majesty and authority and an acknowledgment of his own limited understanding. The Lord had yet to restore what Satan had taken from Job, yet this humble man utters one of the most powerful testimonies of God in Scripture: "I had heard of you by the hearing of the ear, but now my eye sees you" (42:5).

God's boundaries on Job's suffering, and ours, serve a profound purpose. They show that while we undergo tremendous hardship, God remains in control and is aware of the precise extent of our pain. These boundaries show that suffering, though often inexplicable, is never random. And they show that even if God allows death, we and our loved ones who knew Him are still in His tender care. After all, God allowed the death of His own Son. Our hope cannot lie in what will or won't happen. Our hope, like Job's, must remain in God and His greater plan.

Progress Report

Let's take a moment now to look back at how far we've come:

- We started by identifying the bedrock of our personal forest: a steadfast belief that despite our limited comprehension, God reigns supreme and His goodness endures.
- Within the depths of our own forest, we've gained a richer understanding, an intimate recognition, of both the beauty and the frailties growing within.
- Through exploration, we've unraveled the purposes of the fire, which are bordered by God's profound promises.
- And by drawing intentional boundaries, we've contained the flames, eliminating the threat of wildfire.

At this juncture, I trust that a promise of hope is sprouting forth from the seeds cracked open by the heat shock of your suffering. Now we get to explore what's beginning to grow from our charred landscape. Now we have the chance to discover the beauty emerging from the ashes.

IMAGINE: Is there anywhere you sense the embers of your blaze gaining strength? Do you feel the gusts of winds from the outside world fanning those flames, pushing them beyond control? Can you identify the places where you need to draw hard-and-fast boundary lines? Is anyone inadvertently trampling the firebreaks you've already etched into your landscape?

Perhaps, without realizing it, you're adding fuel to your own fire. Consider the kindling you gather as you consume certain news or entertainment and think deeply about how it feeds or extinguishes the flames. Remember, controlled burns are not accidents. So, as you look within, ask yourself, "Where could intentionality serve me well?"

FIREPROOF FAITH

The ash that now covers your forest—the ground that appears so lifeless—holds the miracle of growth. Twenty-five percent of wood ash is calcium carbonate, a nutrient that increases the pH of soil, creating an environment ripe for growth. Ash also contains potassium and phosphate, not to mention important micronutrients like zinc, iron, boron, manganese, and copper.[1]

As the fire in your forest halts at its boundaries and the flames weaken, you'll begin to see what is left behind. Loss and destruction are undeniable, of course. Yet the potential for new growth runs deep. Maybe you're already witnessing tiny sprouts pushing through the ash, daring to reach for the light. You might find yourself questioning the status quo or longing for a deeper, more intimate walk with Jesus. Maybe the allure of past promises is gone. Perhaps religion itself feels fraudulent.

Already, subtle signs of renewal could be emerging from your loss, but they can easily escape notice if your focus remains fixated solely on the ruins. Faith has to look forward, even as it acknowledges what is and what has been.

Names in Light

Grace Anna, Joshua Michael, Tyler, Hope, Lilia Sarah, Devon Thomas, 9/15/1998, Baby Bennet. . . . The colossal screen behind me displayed thousands of names—babies who never lived long enough to learn what their names were. With bated breath, I stood near the front of the church, beholding the sight of hundreds of people streaming in, finding their seats, some clutching a blanket or a keepsake. My gaze shifted to Emma's photograph, perfectly positioned on an easel beside the podium. A bittersweet dance of grief and gratitude overwhelmed my heart as I reflected on what had brought me to this moment.

Throughout my pregnancy, countless parents affected by the loss of their own babies reached out to me. An overwhelming consensus emerged: deep-seated and unresolved grief. For many, the loss of a child in infancy is isolating and lonely. Even well-meaning family and friends mostly tend to stay quiet, perhaps fearing they will inadvertently stir up their loved one's pain. It's an understandable reaction, but it yields a consequence: these little ones remain unacknowledged by the world at large.

As I shared with Cole some of the many stories, we made an easy decision. We resolved to open Emma's memorial to the public, to transform it into a sanctuary for all those who had lost their children. Anyone burdened by the death of a baby was invited to submit the name of his or her child or a significant date.

The floodgates opened and stories poured forth, revealing an astonishing truth: there were mothers who had never uttered their child's name aloud or seen it written, let alone in lights for all to see. I watched as parents pointed out their child's names, simultaneously smiling and crying. It was at once an indescribable ache and a shimmering beacon of hope.

When the moment came for me to share, I opened with a story from years before. I was out to dinner with a group, a few friends but mostly acquaintances, when the conversation turned to a recent tragedy in our city. A church bus accident had claimed the lives of three people from a congregation, including the pastor's son and his pregnant wife. I had reported live from the scene, and part of my heart was still there during this evening out.

The group acknowledged the scope of the tragedy with a collective murmur. Then somebody mentioned a statement released by the grieving pastor and his wife. I knew it was rooted in the couple's unwavering faith, but some of the people at this dinner were skeptical. These parents expressed a profound conviction that their loved ones would not wish to return to this world, for they now resided in a realm free of suffering. Their family members were with Jesus, they explained, experiencing the very promises given to them by the Scriptures. To honor the legacy of their loved ones, this man and woman said they had made a conscious choice to accept the divine plan set forth by God.

It was an incredible statement. I remember being in awe of their faith when the news station received it. However, on that evening at the restaurant, just a week after the incident, one of the men casually dismissed the pastor's conviction as mere "delusion." He asserted that embracing such a narrative was simply how this couple navigated their loss. In his view, clinging to a fabrication, a lie, was a necessity for survival.

Time seemed to stop for me as his words hung in the air, freezing my very being. The pastor was not deluded. In fact, in his suffering, he had gained a clarity that surpassed us all. I was sure of it.

As my internal voices of belief and doubt engaged in an intense battle, I aimlessly picked at my salad. My heart raced, torn between the urge to rise in defense of the pastor's profound faith and the realization that I barely knew most of the people present. Plus, I had never lost a child, so what did I know?

With that last thought, I allowed the doubt to win. The conversation took a turn, and there I sat with an uneaten salad and a heart full of remorse.

The Forging of Belief

What was really behind my hesitance? Frankly, it was unbelief.

Throughout His earthly existence, Jesus implored His audience to do something we naively assume would require no urging: believe. Consider His familiar words in John 3:16: "God so loved the world, that he gave his only Son, that whoever believes in him should not perish but have eternal life." Then we have Jesus's direct statement to Martha: "I am the resurrection and the life. Whoever believes in me, though he die, yet shall he live, and everyone who lives and believes in me shall never die. Do you believe this?" (John 11:25–26). And also His tender words to His disciples ahead of His impending death: "Let not your hearts be troubled. Believe in God; believe also in me" (14:1).

Interesting, isn't it? We often perceive belief as an innate conviction that a person either possesses or lacks. Is that true, or do you and I actually hold the reins of control on our beliefs?

Jesus could have emphasized that His followers study Scripture, perform good deeds, or adhere to ancient laws. Yet time and again, He fervently implores us to believe. To wholeheartedly embrace the power of faith.

How do we do that? We need the Holy Spirit's prompting, coupled with a recognition of our own insufficiency and a steadfast conviction that only Jesus has everything we need.

Acknowledging our weakness can be difficult in times of abundance. That's why suffering holds such tremendous potential: suffering can unveil truth and forge our belief unlike any time of contentment.

This is also why people fear the fire: they don't want anything evaporating their bubble of comfort and self-sufficiency. They'd rather believe what they want to believe and live by their own reality. Sadly, these are the ones who get burned or permanently displaced by the fire. Rather than seeking to rebuild on the burned-out land, plenty of people move away, abandoning their faith. Or they become hardened by hardship rather than being forged by it.

The physical process of forging is truly remarkable. Subjected to intense heat, metal yields under compressive forces, becoming soft and malleable. Once the desired form is achieved, the metal is gradually cooled, increasing its strength and durability.

Our faith can undergo the same process through the crucible of suffering. God uses our hardships to shape us into His intended design and strengthen our belief to a degree that many would deem "delusional." In fact, seeing people living out their faith while their lives are on fire can make others feel vulnerable. Witnessing how their belief sustains them and makes them strong as steel in the flames forces the people around them to face the reality of their own faith or lack thereof. It's easier to criticize someone than to confront what's lacking in your own forest.

The Pharisees had this reaction toward many whose faith came alive through suffering: the woman with uncontrollable bleeding who received healing; the Roman centurion whose beloved servant was restored to health through his plea; the woman at the well whose hidden deeds Jesus revealed; Mary Magdalene, plagued by demons; and Zacchaeus, steeped in corruption. These people encountered Jesus amid disease, deceit, demons, depression, and despair, and it was through their suffering that Jesus met them, healed them . . . and called on them to believe.

The Slow Burn of Long-suffering

Nowhere is the call for belief more important than in long-suffering. It's one thing to experience the rushing flames that roar through a sudden trial. It's another to live among flames that seem to have no end.

For a half century now, a small town in Pennsylvania has endured an ongoing underground inferno. It started back in 1962, possibly when an above-ground fire found its way into one of the town of Centralia's coal mines. Despite numerous attempts to combat the relentless blaze, the fire continued to rage, forcing the eventual evacuation of the town. As time passed, the hopes of extinguishing the fire dwindled, leading authorities to reluctantly accept that the flames were likely to persist and torment the area for many more years to come.

The enduring torment of a slow burn lies in its relentless uncertainty. Even the cruelest agony of death offers certainty, a finality in which one knows: *It's time to begin healing; it's time to push forward. There's no reason to hold on to hope for a different outcome.* But those in the throes of long-suffering trudge painfully through the ambiguous in-between with a constant adjustment of expectations. Questions always accompany this trial:

Is this the worst of it?

Have I done enough?

Should I stop fighting? Should I feel guilty for wondering?

I've talked to people who are enduring a Centralia-type fire in their lives, and they tell me it's essential to climb above the theoretical questions that can cloud belief—questions like, "Does God cause suffering, or does He merely allow it? Why would He even allow it?" They must ascend to the summit, where pain can be seen through a much wider panorama of God's love and care. That's where, even in the most exhausting circumstances, the reality of His goodness gives the incredible gift of rest to a weary soul.

———————

For Melody and her husband, Rob, it's been quite some time since they've experienced life fire-free. Their spark ignited when Melody's widowed father received the crushing diagnosis of Alzheimer's. As her parents' only child, Melody made the difficult decision to leave her job and move in with her dad, who lived five hours away, to become his primary caregiver. Meanwhile, Rob continued to work full-time, trying to carve out a semblance of normalcy within the chaos. Every Thursday at noon, he'd drive to be with his wife and her ailing father, work remotely on Fridays, and return home on Sunday nights. This demanding routine lasted fourteen months. Their lives were a maze of disrupted schedules, sleepless nights, and the unrelenting stress of the unknown, until her father's passing from an aneurysm.

They'd barely had the chance to catch their breath when, just one month later, they received a devastating phone call from Rob's brother: "Mom was killed in a car accident this morning." Soon after came the biggest eruption of all: Rob was diagnosed with an aggressive form of bone cancer that had already metastasized. The pain became so excruciating he could barely move. In the dark hours just days before his first surgery to remove the largest malignant mass, Melody awoke to a heart-wrenching sight: her usually tough, no-nonsense husband weeping on the couch in their living room, demoralized and debilitated by the pain.

While Rob has responded well to treatment, they've been told that except for a miracle, he has maybe five years to live.

Their fire continues to burn. Yet during this long season of searing heat, something miraculous has happened: Rob and Melody's belief that Jesus is guiding them through the flames is more resolute than ever. Even their marriage is stronger than it's been in years.

Long-suffering challenges those in its throes to rally patient endurance to get through one day at a time. Those who prioritize seeking Jesus gain the ability to see situations from His vantage point and recognize even more clearly how close He is.

Jesus implores us to believe, regardless of suffering. We don't always discover the precise solutions or the end to our pain exactly as we pray for it. Yet in the fire of suffering, we find that our capacity for belief expands in profound measure—which, in turn, creates an unshakable faith.

I Believe; Help My Unbelief!

One of my favorite exchanges recorded in the Bible transpires between Jesus and a father in the throes of suffering (see Mark 9:17–27). This man's son has long been plagued by a debilitating spirit that rendered him mute and has afflicted him with seizures since childhood. The spirit is violent, often endangering the boy's life. The father says to Jesus, "If you can do anything, have compassion on us and help us."

Jesus answers, "'If you can'! All things are possible for one who believes."

The father's subsequent reply deeply moves me because I can empathize with both his self-doubt and his desire: "Immediately the father of the child cried out and said, 'I believe; help my unbelief!'" Jesus then rebukes the unclean spirit and raises the boy to new life.

I believe; help my unbelief! What a powerful prayer for us all. Belief does not require that we eradicate all doubt. No, belief is a deliberate choice, a sacred commitment to take Jesus at His word. It means trusting that where and when doubt teases our understanding and challenges our convictions, we have a Savior who is bigger. Spending time with Him will assure us of that truth. And ultimately, true belief will transform us in every aspect of our existence.

In my personal landscape, belief was the tree that regrew the fastest for me. Where a midsized maple had formerly stood, a giant redwood was now emerging . . . unshakable, undeterred, majestic. This tree wouldn't bend to the winds of the world.

When I looked at my life, I couldn't help but be encouraged—not only at this redwood of belief but at the sight of the beautiful tree I saw growing beside it, a tree already green with hope.

Hope

Hope does seem delusional to those without belief. The stirring inside that doesn't make sense considering the circumstances, the conviction that there's more to the story—this stirring is profound and powerful . . . and also incredibly vulnerable to counterfeit.

No wonder the man at our group dinner was skeptical.

We have all assigned such trivial meaning to hope. "I hope there's a parking spot." "I hope it doesn't rain." We have unwittingly shrunk the "sure and steadfast anchor of the soul" into a positive outlook. We have unknowingly morphed the cardinal virtue that "enters into the inner place behind the curtain, where Jesus has gone as a forerunner on our behalf" (Hebrews 6:19–20) into mere wishful thinking. No wonder many have come to view hope as a feeble attempt to just get through the misery of life. Nineteenth-century German philosopher Arthur Schopenhauer went as far as to call hope a form of delusion that deceives us into thinking future conditions will bring lasting happiness. Ultimately, Schopenhauer argued, hope itself is the source of suffering and dissatisfaction.[2]

How has the virtue of hope, attributed to God Himself, come to be viewed as a cheery outlook at best and a deceptive psychological condition at worst? Is hope foolish or an invaluable gift from God? The answer is simple when we realize the world holds two entirely different definitions, like diamonds and glitter. Both sparkle, but one is worth a great price and the other is just a decoration that, depending on the circumstance, can be annoying.

Glittery hope is simply optimism. Most people appreciate a positive outlook. Optimism is applauded, and rightly so. But it's no substitute for diamond-quality hope that has been formed under pressure.

Whereas real hope runs deep, optimism's roots sit just beneath the surface. With just a tug of turmoil, optimism is unearthed and shaken. That's why we see such cynicism toward the notion of hope; optimism cannot save.

The Anchor of the Soul

So, what is hope? And how can we, as Paul prays, "overflow with hope" (Romans 15:13 NIV)?

Genuine hope is based on the indestructibility of truth. We live in an age where truth is said to be fluid, where "your truth" may not be mine. This creates psychological chaos because truth is truth—it cannot change from one person to another. If our hope isn't harbored in the gospel truth, we have no anchor for our souls. Instead, our hope will get blown about by the winds of time. *Today I'm hoping in this idea . . . tomorrow in this person . . . and the next day, in this movement.* The results will always disappoint. They can never withstand the flames of adversity, and they will ultimately lead to a heart grown over with cynicism. That's what's going on when, in the face of suffering, you see some Christians question or leave their faith.

Meanwhile, others find a stronger and richer faith. What's the difference? How you grieve—with or without hope. To despair is to grieve without hope. Those who walk away from their faith during trial have not absorbed truth enough for it to produce hope.

During World War II, as air raid sirens wailed, British minister W. E. Sangster often preached to his congregation in a bomb shelter beneath his church. Once, amid the chaos, Sangster urged those listening to cling tightly to truth, especially in the face of suffering:

Truth is mighty. It does not achieve its victories by any lightning war. The lie wins all early engagements, and sometimes seems to be in the secure possession of the field. The Truth may even be nailed to a cross and taken down, a poor bleeding clod, to be hidden in a sepulchre, sealed with a great stone. But it rises again! The life-principle in it cannot be killed. Somehow, it partakes of the life of God and, therefore, of God's eternity. Ultimately, its triumph is sure.[3]

Hope is powerful because it enduringly and excitedly reminds us of the greatest truth of all time: God is who He says He is, and every longing inside of us will find its satisfaction at Christ's return.

As Christians, hope should be our defining trait—our identifier—setting us apart in a world burdened by sorrow. It is the meaningful offering we get to extend to those drowning in despair. A light in the darkness, a city on a hill, a tree flourishing.

Peter wrote in 1 Peter 1:3–5, "According to his great mercy, [God the Father] has caused us to be born again to a living hope through the resurrection of Jesus Christ from the dead, to an inheritance that is imperishable, undefiled, and unfading, kept in heaven for you, who by God's power are being guarded through faith for a salvation ready to be revealed in the last time." The wisdom of the world disorients us, but what a great relief to be able to stand firm on the hope of the truth of Christ's gospel. Faith is exactly this: "the assurance of things hoped for, the conviction of things not seen" (Hebrews 11:1). It's not wishful thinking, and it's not a positive perspective. It is confidence rooted in truth. And we are promised that *this* hope will never disappoint us (Romans 5:5 CSB).

Do-Over

I wish I could do it again, that dinner years ago. If I could go back and sit with those people, knowing what I know now—having lost what I've lost, having gained what I've gained—I wouldn't try to dispute that man as I long wished I had. I wouldn't try to win over the table or back anyone into a corner. In response to the accusation about the pastor's delusion, I think I would take a page from Jesus's book instead. In kindness, I think I would ask the man a question that might have stayed with him long after our meal. A question that could cut through his cynicism and pierce his heart: "What if the pastor is right?"

What if the profound promises of God are true? What if there really is a divine plan set forth by our Creator? What if those who pass truly wouldn't want to return? What if there is so much more to reality than our earthly existence? What if the deepest pain holds the most divine promise?

What if . . . what if . . . God really is with us?

IMAGINE: Take a moment to look around. What do you see growing from the ashy soil? Is it new to your forest, or perhaps a stronger, more resilient variety of something you've known before? Even if there is no tangible sign, can you discern the desires planted deep within your soul? Consider the poignant words of the psalmist who, in the middle of his own desperation and longing, cries, "Deep calls to deep" (Psalm 42:7).

The deep can feel daunting, new, and uncertain. The shallows feel safer. Yet precisely there, in the depth of sorrow, we will encounter the depth of God—His provision, His abundance, His unfathomable love. This depth, in turn, beckons us to greater faith and profound hope.

Where is God calling you deeper? Are you willing to go?

FIREPOWER

In the tender months following Emma's death, I couldn't shake this curiosity: *What happened to me in the hospital room that morning of our release? What was the overwhelming surge of power that coursed through my body? The profound peace, weighty with significance?* I didn't have a clear answer, but I knew in a general sense it was the presence of God. And I now had an insatiable hunger for more.

I thought back to one small group of people in a budding church who, during my pregnancy, had kindly offered to pray over Cole and me. We had respectfully declined. But slowly, throughout our journey, we got to know some of these individuals, and they were ... different. They prayed with power. Their belief wasn't bound. I was captivated and curious. There was a peculiar semblance between them and my encounter in the hospital room, but I couldn't quite connect the dots. All I knew was, I wanted to find out.

Driven mostly by a deep gratitude for their unwavering support, we decided to visit their church one Sunday. Within the first few minutes, it struck me like a bolt of ethereal lighting. Once again, I sensed that same sensation, that same surge of power, here within these walls. Or was it within these people? It wasn't that they had it all together. Their focus wasn't on themselves, yet it seemed as if they were propelled by divine horsepower. Cole and I walked out of church that Sunday with a resolute certainty gripping each of us: God was unveiling a new path before us in the emerging regrowth of our forests, and there was no turning back.

For most of my childhood, I found myself wrapped in the embrace of a remarkable Christian family. Both my parents assumed positions of leadership within our church, which became our second home in many ways. Many of my memories and friendships took root at Pioneer Girls every Wednesday night. Sunday mornings, when my brother and I weren't trying to make each other laugh at the choir leader's exaggerated vibrato, we learned about God.

In those formative years, my young mind filled with the gift of sound biblical teaching. Sound, but perhaps not complete. Our trinity seemed to consist of God the Father, the Son, and the Holy Scriptures. Of course, this was never explicitly stated, but the Holy Spirit always seemed to be an afterthought—an obscure third angle of the Trinity or perhaps the oddball cousin no one knows what to do with. I grew up skeptical of anything involving the supernatural workings of the Holy Spirit. The term "charismatic"— despite having too many letters—practically seemed like a four-letter word.

As I grew up into my own personal faith, I learned to acknowledge the Holy Spirit, but I still didn't have a healthy understanding of Him or the profound gift of His presence. My former forest, filled with judgment and fear of man, hindered any full revelation of Him. But here I was now, in the middle years of my life, standing amid the remnants of what once was, with dense thickets of pride and self-righteousness reduced to heaps of ash. My biblical foundation was laid bare yet buried under dead vegetation; something exciting was taking root; a panoramic vista of truth was unfolding before me. "There's more," I said to Cole as we got in our car one Sunday afternoon.

"I know," he responded, both of us lost in the view that lay before us.

From Basement Low to Hilltop High

I gained my first real glimpse of this in my junior year of college. Emotionally drained one day, I found myself on the hard basement floor of my apartment, feeling as though I had fallen off a spiritual tightrope—something I'd delicately walked during my teen and young adult years. I had dedicated my life to Jesus at the tender age of five and can still vividly remember the surge of chills as I made that commitment.

However, despite my deep love for Jesus, a streak of rebellion always cohabitated with my natural fear of authority. I was drawn to excitement and fun and repulsed by rules that I deemed controlling. Conventional and straitlaced guys bored me. I would start many a night at youth group, only to finish at a party, drinking cheap beer and smoking Marlboro Menthol Lights. I carried this dual life—laden with fun times and always a tinge of remorse—into college.

At Temple University in Philadelphia, where I pursued broadcast journalism, my fake ID saw far more use than my Bible. I didn't realize at the time that I was partying with a purpose. In a very roundabout way, I was looking for love. It had been seven years since my parents' unexpected divorce turned my world upside down. I refused to place my trust in anything or anyone that might disappoint, yet ironically, being able to trust someone's love was exactly what I craved.

Midway through my junior year, I had grown weary of the college party scene and was spiritually famished.

I felt empty, used, and overlooked by the world I had chased for so long. I knew what I needed, who I needed, but I had kept Him at a distance for so long now. Finally, in my basement apartment, my need outweighed any neglect. In desperation, I collapsed on the floor and wept. All the unmet expectations and the sadness of a life that hadn't unfolded as I'd imagined overwhelmed me. In that moment, Jesus met me, enveloping me with supernatural peace and, I knew, immediate forgiveness. On that floor, as the flames of failure roared through, He planted a seed of hunger in my heart. I became insatiable for the things of God.

I devoured a forty-day devotional my mom had sent me, which had been gathering dust until then. I was profoundly thankful for Jesus and His rescue and incredibly excited about my future. I wanted to surrender everything, but being a broke college student, all I had to offer was the week of spring break that was approaching. I vowed to give it to Him.

I researched dozens of mission trips, hoping to use my week off for a greater purpose. None fit within my time frame. With reluctance, I turned down offers of beachside vacations and resolved to return home to Lancaster, Pennsylvania, for the week. I'd work at Water Street Mission if nothing else.

A few weeks before my break, my mom called me one afternoon. "I know there's no way you'll want to do this," she began. I sat my ramen down, anticipating what was next. ". . . but my church is sending out a group for a mission trip and they have two spots open." The dates were the exact dates of my break. "Yes!" I blurted out. "Let's go!"

As I soared above the clouds to Guadalajara, Mexico, a smile played on my lips. Could God truly be this intricately involved in the details of my life? Was He actively answering the cries of my heart? Was He genuinely this fun? A resounding *Yes!* echoed from the depths of my heart.

That week in Mexico, I worked at a Youth With A Mission base, scraping layers of old paint off cabinets. There was nothing especially moving about the trip, but I felt profoundly fulfilled. From my place of desperation, shoots of hope and purpose sprouted within me. On the last day of my week, I climbed a nearby hill and stretched my arms toward the heavens. With a cry resonating from deep inside, I exclaimed, "Use me!" I didn't know precisely what I was asking God for in that moment, but I knew it was why I was created. I knew there could be nothing more fulfilling.

From With to Within

Before Jesus's imminent crucifixion, He tried to convey to His disciples that His departure would ultimately be for their advantage. Emmanuel—the divine gift of *God with us*—stood before His determined followers, assuring them it's better that He leave.

Can you imagine the confusion that must have gripped those men? Jesus elaborated by revealing that if He did not go, the Helper could not come to them. "But if I go," He said, "I will send him to you" (see John 16:4–7).

Have you ever found yourself entertaining the thought, *If only I could walk beside Jesus, how much simpler this journey would be?* The disciples *were* with Jesus. They reveled in friendship—sharing meals, traveling together, and witnessing wondrous miracles. Yet on the night of His betrayal, every single one of them, despite their ardent affection, abandoned Him. Their love for Him, genuine as it was, proved to be tethered to limitations and overshadowed by uncertainty and doubt.

Jesus was intimately acquainted with human fragility, and that's the reason He so urgently wanted to convey a profound revelation to His chosen: "He [the Spirit of truth] will glorify me, for he will take what is mine and declare it to you. All that the Father has is mine; therefore I said that he will take what is mine and declare it to you" (vv. 14–15).

In that moment, Jesus shared with these men the most extraordinary concept to have ever graced humanity. He informed them that His very Spirit would be imparted to them—His power, His wisdom, His intimate connection with the Father. Soon, all of this would be theirs!

The disciples didn't understand.

After Jesus's resurrection, He spent forty more days on earth before His ascent to heaven. As His departure drew near, He again delivered a significant message to His disciples, urging them to remain in Jerusalem and await the promised gift from the Father. He reminded them that while John the Baptist had baptized with water, a baptism of an entirely different nature awaited them—a baptism of the Holy Spirit, an immersion in divine power just days away. "The Holy Spirit will come upon you, and you will be seized with power" (Acts 1:8 TPT).

With these words resonating in their hearts, Jesus departed, leaving the disciples in a state of bewilderment. For the ensuing ten days, approximately 120 people gathered, unified by their shared hope. Then, at long last, the appointed day of Pentecost arrived—a day that would forever alter the course of their lives and ours. A remarkable event unfolded, defying any boundaries of logic and comprehension. "Suddenly there came from heaven a sound like a mighty rushing wind, and it filled the entire house where they were sitting. And divided tongues as of fire appeared to them and rested on each one of them. And they were all filled with the Holy Spirit and began to speak in other tongues as the Spirit gave them utterance" (Acts 2:2–4).

Consider the implausibility of this, but also the humanity: that rushing wind, that ethereal fire. Although these were new sensations, they must have contained an air of familiarity. It was none other than the Spirit of their Savior, their Lord, their cherished companion. The very same Spirit who had astonished them through Jesus's profound questions posed to the Pharisees; the very same Spirit who had triumphantly raised Lazarus from the clutches of death; the very same Spirit who had withstood a forty-day temptation—this Spirit now resided in them.

And what transpired next? A once-regret-ridden Peter fearlessly addressed the people of Israel with resounding power and resolve. Men and women in droves came to believe. Signs and wonders appeared regularly. Those hesitant disciples, now indwelt by the Spirit of God, transformed into steadfast and authoritative witnesses, unwavering pillars of strength, as they proclaimed the gospel. Not once do we hear of any faltering among the disciples for the remainder of their lives!

How can that possibly be? When Jesus said, "It is better I leave you," He meant it. You see, while Jesus had walked among them, the disciples had carried a limited measure of authority—able to cast out demons and perform miraculous healings—but they had lacked the unshakable power that awaited them. The arrival of the Holy Spirit unlocked a level of steadfast pursuit previously unknown to them. The once uncertain became resolute, the faltering became firm, and the vacillating became veracious witnesses to the gospel.

In your vulnerability, consider: Which form of the disciples' existence resonates with you? Before you dismiss their miraculous turnaround as something set apart just for them, let's look at another account.

Shortly after Pentecost, a man named Apollos played a significant role in spreading the message of Jesus during the early years of the first century AD. The Scriptures describe this Jewish believer as a man of eloquence and knowledge, hailing from the renowned city of Alexandria, a hub of intellectual and cultural pursuits. He was described as "mighty in the Scriptures" and "fervent in spirit" (Acts 18:24–25 NASB1995), teaching accurately about Jesus.

Impressive, one might say. Yet there was a caveat. The account reveals that Apollos possessed knowledge solely of John's baptism, unaware of the full revelation of the gospel.

It came to pass that while Apollos was fervently speaking in the synagogue, a couple named Priscilla and Aquila, dear friends of Paul, were in the congregation. As they listened to Apollos's words, they recognized that he had not yet fully grasped the gospel. With compassion and love, they took this fervent teacher aside and explained to him the way of God more accurately. A humble Apollos, his spirit open and receptive, gratefully received their gentle correction. The church community rallied around him, eager to uplift him as he expanded his ministry. Truly, it's a moving scene of humility and human connection— the type of caring and connection that should always typify the church.

I wonder if Paul got wind of this encounter, because in the next chapter of Acts, he comes through Corinth, finds a group of disciples, and immediately asks, "Did you receive the Holy Spirit when you believed?"

They responded, "No, we have not even heard that there is a Holy Spirit."

"Into what then were you baptized?" asked Paul.

"Into John's baptism."

So, Paul clarifies, "John baptized with the baptism of repentance, telling the people to believe in the one who was to come after him, that is, Jesus."

On hearing this, reports Luke, "they were baptized in the name of the Lord Jesus. And when Paul had laid his hands on them, the Holy Spirit came on them, and they began speaking in tongues and prophesying" (see Acts 19:1–6).

When Everything Changed

God's Word is clear that the Holy Spirit dwells deep within every person who embraces faith in Jesus Christ. In fact, the Bible tells us belief without the Holy Spirit is impossible. However, what we see in this context is that a person can indeed hold belief while lacking the transformative power poured out through the baptism of the Holy Spirit. I know there are conflicting theologies that cloud this topic, and my intention is not to play theologian. What I can offer, though, is my story. So here it is.

When Cole and I began stepping into unknown waters, inviting the Holy Spirit into our lives in greater measure . . . when we deliberately created space for Him to convict and correct us . . . when we earnestly pursued His various gifts . . . when we exalted Him to His rightful place as an equal person within the three-in-one of the Trinity . . . when we willfully set aside our skepticism and got to know Him, not as the oddball cousin but as our greatest Advocate . . . everything changed.

Gone were the days of lukewarm devotion, where we found ourselves riding the tumultuous roller coaster of faith, perpetually wrestling with stubborn, recurrent sin and plagued by lingering doubts. Instead, we emerged as more confident followers of Jesus, empowered to break the bonds of sin, emboldened to approach the throne of grace, and on fire to grow in our giftings for the edification of the church. Moves of God became common in our lives. Even today, Cole and I often find ourselves teary-eyed, reveling in God's extravagance, astounded by how intimately the Holy Spirit knows and cares for us.

In my suffering and vulnerability, I discovered the answer to a profound longing: my craving to fully embrace my position as a child of God. No longer could I reduce the Holy Spirit to a mere doctrinal dispute. He is a person. He is God. He is limitless in power. He is present everywhere. He knows all the truths of God and all the mysteries of God. He leads us into deeper communion with Jesus. He is eternal. *He is with us.*

The enemy's headstrong pursuit to cause confusion and division around the Holy Spirit makes sense to me now. If I were trying to tame the cosmic power of Christ's bride, that's what I would go after too.

Satan knows the catastrophic consequence that would ensue if Christians awakened to the full potential and authority given to them through the Holy Spirit. The Spirit operates as the fire, the wind, and the breath of God! A force unstoppable would be unleashed—a resurgence of the church, reclaiming its intended place. Denominational differences would fade to insignificance; worship styles and building aesthetics would be rendered inconsequential. The Holy Spirit holds the key—the very heartbeat of our faith, the nucleus of our existence.

A Supernatural Surge

Martyn Lloyd-Jones, a Welsh Protestant minister and medical doctor, was an influential Calvinist in the British evangelical movement in the twentieth century. In *Joy Unspeakable*, a masterful collection of his sermons, the minister dissects two dangers that surround our understanding and pursuit of the Holy Spirit.

The first lies in straying beyond the boundaries of scriptural truth in our zealous quest for personal experiences—using manipulation or coercion to manufacture experience. From this danger stems most of the skepticism toward the pursuit of the Holy Spirit, and rightly so.

Lloyd-Jones next shines a light on a contrasting concern that ensnares far more people, which he considered the "greater danger of the two." It's "the exact opposite of the first," he wrote, "as these things generally go from one violent extreme to the other. How difficult it always is to maintain a balance! The second danger . . . is that of being satisfied with something very much less than what is offered in the Scripture, and the danger of interpreting Scripture by our experiences and reducing its teaching to the level of what we know and experience."[1]

For all our avowed belief in an outrageous God, we Christians tend to be awfully skittish about the supernatural. I still wrestle with an inclination to doubt. I read about Moses's extraordinary encounter with the burning bush, Jacob's wrestling match with God, and Jesus's terrifying expulsion of demons into a herd of pigs. I admire David's undignified dancing in the streets and Mary's audacious act of anointing Jesus's feet with costly oil, using her own hair. Yet in the depths of my heart, I have silently passed judgment on others' personal encounters with God. I've cast a skeptical side-eye at the person sprawled on the floor in fervent worship. Dancing before God in public? *Let's not draw attention to ourselves.*

Admittedly, these examples are outward expressions, whereas the most profound work of the Holy Spirit takes place internally, in the secret place. However, I use these instances to uncover our hesitations, the veils we have woven and erected to keep certain facets of God's presence at a safe distance.

Even before the charismatic movement emerged, Billy Graham recounted a time he spent with Swiss theologian Karl Barth. A curious Graham asked Barth, "What do you think will be the next theological emphasis in the world?"

Barth's response was immediate and direct. "The Holy Spirit."[2]

Now, I obviously can't expand on Barth's answer for him, but I wholeheartedly agree. Here's my reasoning: Many followers of Christ hold the belief that conversion is the ultimate goal. Indeed, we cannot progress without experiencing salvation. Yet to stop there would be to miss the essence of salvation itself. We are saved *so that* we can be filled to the brim, overflowing, saturated in the power of the Holy Spirit. Not often does the Bible relay that Jesus "cried out," but consider the depths of His emotions on the final day of the feast: "Jesus stood up and cried out, 'If anyone thirsts, let him come to me and drink. Whoever believes in me, as the Scripture has said, "Out of his heart will flow rivers of living water."' *Now this he said about the Spirit,* whom those who believed in him were to receive, for as yet the Spirit had not been given, because Jesus was not yet glorified" (John 7:37–39, emphasis mine).

Rivers of living water. Did you happen to picture a river in your forest when you initially envisioned it? Did you think about what happens to a river during a raging inferno? Stripped of its vegetation, a river will surge with increased speed and volume. A faster, more intense flow will barrel through its banks. In your pain, when fire has stripped you of everything, God can unleash a new and profound flow of the Holy Spirit in your life. He can turn a dry creek bed into a river of rushing, living water.

Friends, there is so much more for us. But the Holy Spirit does not impose Himself where He isn't invited. So, I implore you, ask! Ask for more of His presence, more of His comfort, more of His loving conviction. Pursue the gifts of the Spirit that build you up and that in turn build up the church. If you desire more of God, tell the One who generously gives to all, and then get around people whose passion is contagious. People who will ignite and incite you in your pursuit of the Holy Spirit. People who hunger for moves of God, however that happens and whatever that looks like. People who will sharpen you and encourage you prophetically.

After feeling the rush of the river, comfortable Christianity will no longer satisfy. This isn't about emotional experience. This is about the ordained, earthly existence of a Christ follower. You and I have one fleeting opportunity in this life. Let's not reach its end and realize we settled for a penny when God, in His boundless grace, offered us the untold riches of heaven.

IMAGINE: A gentle breeze dances at your back, and you instinctually look up and breathe deeply. The sun warms your face. A smile ever so slightly curves its way skyward too. You don't know if a smile is appropriate given everything that's been lost, but it seems right to return the warmth you're being given. The changes unfolding before your eyes are nothing you ever wanted or imagined, yet somehow, your forest is breathing again. You are breathing again.

Close your eyes and return to the forest you initially imagined at the beginning of this book. What differences do you notice now? What does this place look and sound like? Can you hear the rush of a river carving out a new path, streaming from a waterfall of hunger for God? Can you see a cleared-away panorama of hope that takes your breath away?

Instinctively, you reach for the same scarred hand that guided you through the flames. It now feels deeply familiar. You can't imagine how you navigated the terrain for so long without this Companion by your side. Thankfully, you don't have to walk without Him ever again. An entire lifetime of exploration with Him lies ahead.

CONCLUSION

FROM THE ASHES

As you cautiously begin to walk through your forest again, you notice a feeling you'd long forgotten—the soft padding of grass underneath your feet. It makes you pause, taking in the reality of your renewing landscape. You peer up at the canopy of leaves and then follow their shadows dancing on the path in front of you. A sense of familiarity tugs at you, and yet it's all new.

Your eye catches sight of blackened stumps amid the green canvas, a reminder of the ravaging flames that once consumed this sacred place. There's no denying what transpired. This is a place where gratitude and grief intertwine. A place where each draws strength from the other. A place to cherish what stands tall amid the painful scars of what's gone. There's no demand to move on here, only that invitation you've been clutching. You open it again, now dirtied and worn.

It simply says, "An Invitation to Know Me."

A Consuming Fire

The night before Jesus was crucified, He lifted up His most urgent request to His Father. Aware that death was staring Him down, Jesus pleaded, "Father, I know it's time, but there's something I want. And it's not religion. It's not forty-five minutes on Sunday morning. It's not an obligation. It's not powerless pews. Father, I desire that they also, whom you have given Me, may be with Me where I am, to see My glory that you have given Me because you loved Me before the foundation of the world.

"I want my people to *be with Me.* I want them to be set on fire by My presence, Father! I want them consumed by My goodness! Through suffering, draw them close to Us, Father! Take My life as a sacrifice, but give them My glory!" (see John 17).

God Almighty is a consuming fire. He burns with desire for us, and He will not stand by while the enemy of our souls keeps us unmotivated, unimpressed, and unengaged. Through the pain of our flames, Jesus calls us out—out of ordinary, out of comfortable, out of complacency, out of insignificance, out of confusion, out of emptiness—and invites us to behold Him, the epitome, the majesty and splendor, the embodiment of the fullness of God.

The All-Powerful is unfathomably All-Personal, inviting you, inviting me, *to know Him.* Here and now. In our suffering and grief. To behold His glory and, in turn, to be transformed into people who are tested and true, sifted but saved, refined and ready. A people who walk in holy confidence with promise and power. A people whose fascination and wonder of Him are restored. A people who can show a hurting world that there is an answer to all longing and all despair.

Redemption

Two years after Emma's death, I found myself sitting on our deck one afternoon, my Bible open in my lap. I had taken an extended leave from my job, and I now had time for moments like this. New and increasing anxiety at work had been not-so-subtly delivering me a message that change was coming and I needed time to understand what it meant.

As a gentle breeze caught my attention, I paused to take in the scene before me. My husband and son together in the kayak on our pond, the leaves in the trees gently swaying, birds gliding overhead. I turned to peek at the baby monitor. Our daughter, Marlowe Laine, was napping soundly. This tiny "storyteller" of ours was an astonishing gift of redemption, one that I'd had a hard time embracing for much of my pregnancy. It was as if my mind couldn't comprehend God's goodness.

I had returned to work soon after her birth and was still holding tightly to my job and the paycheck that came with it. But on that sunny afternoon, something shifted, and I knew God was calling me out. Not just out of TV news, but out of my own way. I knew He was calling me to leave the little kingdom I had spent my whole life building, to focus my energies on *His* kingdom. Not only did it not make sense financially, but it was outright crazy. I will always remember Cole's response, and my surprise, when I told him the nudging I felt to leave.

"Do it," he said.

This wasn't the same man who had perpetually questioned his salvation and checked our savings account. I wasn't the same person either.

When our forests were first lit ablaze, I truly believed God was sending a message to the world through our little Emma—a message I already knew at surface level: that He is with us. I now understand the message was intended for me; the fact that He is with us . . . should change everything. Today, Emmanuel is an ever-unfolding revelation, an invaluable gift I unwrap every day. Whereas I used to think the gospel of Jesus was a belief system you learned and accepted, full stop, I now realize I was missing the astonishing depth, the cosmic scope, the mind-blowing inheritance that is ours right here and right now. Like the entrancing dance of flames in a fire, which are more amazing the longer you stare, the gospel of Jesus Christ will eternally reveal new and astounding facets of truth to those who dare to behold it. To those who linger and long to truly see.

Cleared and Cultivated

Cole and I didn't know how we would make things work once I quit my job, but we knew we could trust God.

We were both different people. Our former forests had been cleared and new growth was now being cultivated. The fire of Emma's death had burned nearly everything. Our hearts still ache for Emma, and as much as Marlowe is a gift to our family, our redemption didn't come from just replacing what was lost. (It never does.) Suffering's true redemption is knowing Jesus. It's a greater capacity for the things of God. It's the deep assurance that He *really* is with us. It's King David's admission, "My suffering was good for me" (Psalm 119:71 NLT).

It's true that I was the vessel through whom Emmanuel brought Emma Noel into this world, but here's a profound truth: through Emma, Emmanuel delivered me.

Mary Magdalene

Perhaps the greatest biblical example of a controlled burn comes in the form of another deliverance, the life of Mary Magdalene.

The description in Luke's Gospel of Mary's tumultuous past makes it clear that a wildfire had long been ravishing her personal forest: "Mary, called Magdalene, from whom seven demons had gone out" (8:2).

Jesus meets this tormented soul in the middle of unimaginable circumstances, calls her name, and rescues her from the clutches of darkness. Immediate release— from misery to mercy, from captivity to freedom. We don't know the extent of the horror she endured in life, but I suspect that imagining a ghastly existence would not be too much.

We don't know if Mary knew of Jesus before He came to her rescue. We don't know how the demons reacted to the proximity of God Himself when Jesus drew near to her. What we do know is that she was radically changed, her wildfire immediately extinguished at the presence of Jesus.

She stays close to Him. She's unwavering. She's there for His teachings, His miracles, His acts of compassion. She tends to His needs and to His heart. She's not only profoundly grateful to the one who freed her from the tormenting flames, but she loves her Messiah deeply. And when the tables turn, as darkness envelops Jesus in His most trying hour and all but one of His closest disciples turns away, Mary stays. She's there at the foot of the cross. She hears His gasps, His pleas to the Father. She watches the same feet she anointed with oil get crushed by hammer and nail. She is with Jesus through to the bitter end, and with His last breath, she watches her entire world die. Another fire ignites in Mary's forest, but this one is different—it's controlled by boundaries, bordered by deep ravines of love.

At her earliest opportunity, Mary returns to the tomb to prepare Jesus's body. Approaching the tomb that Sunday morning, a new wave of grief washes over her. The tomb is empty. Who took His body?

She rushes to tell the other disciples. John and Peter hurry to see for themselves. It's true; it's empty.

The disciples go back home. But again, Mary stays.

When the others leave, she lingers. When the others try to figure out what happened, Mary just weeps. She stoops to look into the tomb again, and now she sees two angels in white, sitting where the body of Jesus had so recently lain. They ask Mary why she's weeping. "They have taken away my Lord, and I do not know where they have laid him," she responds (John 20:13).

She turns around and sees Jesus, but she doesn't know it's Him. Jesus asks her again why she's weeping. He asks her who she's looking for. Thinking this is the gardener, Mary says, "Sir, if you have carried him away, tell me where you have laid him, and I will take him away" (v. 15). In her grief, Mary misses the presence of angels. She misses Jesus. She doesn't remember His promises. She's bought into the lie that because of the suffering, something went wrong.

But then . . . Jesus speaks her name. The same voice that demanded the demons flee. The same voice that cracked jokes around the dinner table. The same voice that always assured her in her doubt. The same way He always said it.

"Mary."

I imagine her pausing for just a second, her heart beginning to beat wildly, before she turns and *sees Him.* "Rabboni!" she exclaims. *My* teacher! She grasps Him, but

Jesus tells her not to cling to Him. He hasn't ascended to the Father yet. Instead: "Go to my brothers," He tells her, "and say to them, 'I am ascending to my Father and your Father, to my God and your God'" (see vv. 16–17).

When Jesus speaks her name, Mary's grief turns to hope. However, there's a problem. Mary is still calling Jesus "Rabbi," not "Lord." She has been looking for the same man who taught them and lived among them, the only Jesus she's known. She's forgotten what Jesus foretold: Something new is coming. Something beyond the scope of any miracle she's already witnessed. The Spirit of Jesus Christ Himself was about to dwell in Mary forever. The intimacy she longed for with Him would soon be reality. *Jesus could not let her cling to the past.*

Mary's controlled burn ushered her into a new story—a wondrous life with the Holy Spirit. Everything changed. A relationship with the Father, once accessed by Jesus alone, now belonged to her and to all who believe. Unfathomable!

From fervent followers of Jesus to His beloved siblings, from awestruck admiration to a wholehearted embracing of sacred authority, a momentous awakening has taken place, and at its heart is Mary, the chosen messenger. "I have seen the Lord" she tells the disciples (v. 18). This very woman once associated with demons, whose charred remains once felt permanent, becomes eternally known as the first witness to the resurrected Christ. The woman who had nothing is now forever immortalized in church history as "an apostle to the apostles." She's esteemed. She's given authority. She's completely new. Mary has seen the risen Lord, and she is now able to tell others the triumphant truth that they, too, can grieve and hope.

In the depths of her yearning for Jesus, in her tears and desperation, Mary's abiding love sets the stage for an encounter that would alter the course of history. In her grief, Jesus doesn't give Mary what she initially wants—a return to normal. He gives her so much more. And He wants to do the same for you and me through our fires. He wants to reveal Himself, to give us a new life and a calling full of purpose.

Forged in the Fire

Jesus is reaching out His hand. To rescue you, yes. But also to pull you higher. To call you up. To promote you to the place where believers have been forged in the fire. To the place beyond the realm of comfortable Christianity where power, freedom, and purpose rule the hearts of all who truly believe.

The world desperately needs Christians who accept Jesus's invitation. It needs courageous kingdom warriors who have come face-to-face with real pain, who have stared death straight in the eyes and gritted their teeth against the oppression of suffering. The world needs believers who have discovered the radical power of God's presence, who have been transformed, renewed, and strengthened.

The world needs you. The world needs your voice. The world needs your testimony that you have walked through fire and you weren't burned.

Your story of sitting with Jesus in suffering.

Your realization that He is so much closer than you could've ever imagined.

Your witness that within the grasp of grief, you found Him worthy of it all.

ACKNOWLEDGMENTS

To my husband, Cole: You have selflessly cheered me, sacrificially supported me, and steadfastly stood by me through every triumph and every tragedy. More than anyone else, you have led me closer to the Father. Being your wife is the greatest honor of my life. I love you, respect you, and am endlessly grateful for you.

To Max and Marlowe: My love for you cannot be contained. Just looking at you fills me with ridiculous amounts of joy and pride. You inspire every decision and motivate every move I make. I pray you continue to flourish in the freedom and abundance of Jesus. There is nothing more worth pursuing. I love you more!

To our family: Thank you for always believing in me and encouraging me to follow the right paths, even when they're offbeat and uncertain. Your love has been a constant source of support and laughter, a wellspring of strength. I am profoundly grateful for each of you.

To Antioch Indy: Your passion for Jesus is irresistible and your love for people is unmistakable. Thank you for coming alongside of us during our darkest hours and never leaving. Your teachings have inspired much of this book, and your unwavering encouragement has given me the confidence to write it. You are more than friends; you are forever family.

To Traders Point Christian Church: Your unparalleled generosity humbles us. We are eternally thankful for your guidance in wisdom and truth, and for celebrating Emma's life with such profound impact.

To our friends: Whether lifelong, recent additions, or somewhere in between, your steadfast friendship means the world to us. We cherish each and every one of you and are deeply grateful for all the ways you've poured out your love and support.

To the Fedd Agency and Dexterity: Thank you for taking a chance on a once-upon-a-time news anchor with a once-in-a-lifetime vision.

ACKNOWLEDGMENTS

To Kris Bearss: Thank you for holding my hand and my heart as we reshaped and reworked this manuscript. I'm still looking forward to that in-person hug.

To my heavenly Father: When we asked for Your glory to be revealed through Emma's life and our story, we could have never imagined the ways You would answer our desperate plea. Thank You for trusting us with this testimony. I pray our lives honor You, King Jesus. You are worthy of it all!

ABOUT THE AUTHOR

Brooke Martin is an Emmy-winning anchor and reporter originally from Lancaster, Pennsylvania. For fifteen years, Brooke told the community's stories and asked the hard questions of those in charge. From an Oval Office interview to a conversation with a neighbor who had just lost his job, Brooke has held a front row seat to both the impressive and the important stories that make up our lives.

But none impacted her more than her own. Shortly after announcing her second pregnancy on air, Brooke and her husband received a fatal diagnosis for their daughter, Emma Noelle. For six months, Brooke carried their daughter while publicly walking through grief and, ultimately, loss.

Brooke is now working to show others how life's fires can bring new growth, greater beauty, and everlasting hope. Sign up for her free resource, Proof + Prayer, sent straight to your inbox from MoreWithBrookeMartin.com.

Brooke lives in Zionsville, Indiana, with her husband, Cole, and her two children, Max and Marlowe. You can find them at their church, Antioch Indy, or biking on one of Zionsville's beautiful trails.

NOTES

Chapter 1

1. Alex Wigglesworth, "Forest Service Resumes Prescribed Fire Program, but Some Fear New Rules Will Delay Projects," *Los Angeles Times*, September 13, 2022, https://www.latimes.com/california/story/2022-09-13/forest-service-resumes-prescribed-burning/.

2. "Sadhu Sundar Singh: The Story of an Indian Saint," *Christian Post*, November 10, 2003, https://www.christianpost.com/news/sadhu-sundar-singh-the-story-of-an-indian-saint.html.

3. Timothy Keller, *Walking with God through Pain and Suffering* (2013; repr., New York: Penguin, 2015), 30.

Chapter 2

1. Max Lucado, *You Are Special* (Wheaton, IL: Crossway, 1997).

2. See Augustine, *Confessions*, vol. 1 of *Basic Writings of St. Augustine*, ed. Whitney J. Oates (New York: Random House, 1948), 1.1.1.

3. C. S. Lewis, *A Mind Awake: An Anthology of C. S. Lewis*, ed. Clyde Kilby (Boston: Mariner, 2003), 86.

Chapter 3

1. Charles Haddon Spurgeon, "Honest Dealing with God" (June 20, 1875), from *Metropolitan Tabernacle Pulpit*, vol. 21, The Spurgeon Center, https://www.spurgeon.org/resource-library/sermons/honest-dealing-with-god/#flipbook/.

2. N. T. Wright, *Simply Good News: Why the Gospel Is News and What Makes It Good* (New York: HarperCollins, 2015), 70.

3. National Council for Behavioral Health, "How to Manage Trauma Infographic," February 5, 2022, available for download on the website of the National Council for Mental Wellbeing, https://www.thenationalcouncil.org/resources/how-to-manage-trauma-2/.

4. Ruth Haley Barton, *Sacred Rhythms: Arranging Our Lives for Spiritual Transformation* (Downers Grove, IL: IVP, 2006), 24.

5. Paraphrased from Timothy Keller, *Walking with God through Pain and Suffering* (London: Penguin Books, 2013), 317.

6. Andrew Murray, *Andrew Murray on Prayer* (New Kensington, PA: Whitaker House, 1998).

Chapter 4

1. Michael Molthan, "Confessions of a Felon," I Am Second, July 19, 2023, https://www.iamsecond.com/film/michael-molthan/#modal-media-vimeo.

2. Dane C. Ortlund, *How Does God Change Us?*, Union (Wheaton, IL: Crossway, 2021), 64.

3. Ortlund, 64–65.

4. Oswald Chambers, *My Utmost for His Highest: Updated Language Paperback (A Daily Devotional with 366 Bible-Based Readings)*, ed. James Reimann (Grand Rapids: Our Daily Bread, 2010), November 1.

Chapter 5

1. C. H. Spurgeon, Sermon 1310: "The Blind Befriended," *The Metropolitan Tabernacle Pulpit: Sermons Preached and Revised*, vol. 22 (London: Passmore and Alabaster, 1877), 473.

2. *The Transforming Power of Suffering: Reflections from the Pentecostal Perspective* (Pentecostal Herald, 1915).

Chapter 6

1. C. H. Spurgeon, Sermon 2301: "Marah Better Than Elim," *The Metropolitan Tabernacle Pulpit: Sermons Preached and Revised*, vol. 39 (London: Passmore, 1893), 151.

2. Paul David Tripp, *New Morning Mercies: A Daily Gospel Devotional* (Wheaton, IL: Crossway, 2014), 1.

3. John Newton, "I Asked the Lord That I Might Grow" (1779). Public domain.

4. C. S. Lewis, excerpt from a letter to Don Giovanni Calabria (August 10, 1938) in *The Quotable Lewis*, ed. Wayne Martindale and Jerry Root (Carol Stream, IL: Tyndale, 1990), 579.

Chapter 7

1. Brené Brown, *The Gifts of Imperfection: Let Go of Who You Think You're Supposed to Be and Embrace Who You Are*, 10th anniversary ed. (New York: Random House, 2020), 97.

2. Lea Winerman, "Suppressing the 'White Bears,'" *Monitor on Psychology*, October 2011, 44, https://www.apa.org/monitor/2011/10/unwanted-thoughts.

3. Leo Tolstoy, *What Is Art?* (Overland Park, KS: Digireads. com, 2020), 39.

4. Brené Brown, *Braving the Wilderness: The Quest for True Belonging and the Courage to Stand Alone* (New York: Random House, 2019), 123.

5. Mary Constantine, "Gatlinburg Man Forgives Teens Accused of Setting Fires That Killed Wife, 2 Daughters," knoxnews.com, December 16, 2016, https://www.knoxnews .com/story/news/local/tennessee/2016/12/16/gatlinburg-man -forgives-teens-accused-setting-fires-killed-wife-2-daughters /95512384/.

Chapter 8

1. "Story Behind the Song: It Is Well with My Soul," *St. Augustine Record*, October 16, 2014, https://www.staugustine. com/story/lifestyle/faith/2014/10/17/story-behind-song-it -well-my-soul/985525007/.

2. Horatio Spafford, "It Is Well with My Soul," 1873. Public domain.

Chapter 9

1. University of Georgia Extension, "Best Management Practices for Wood Ash as Agricultural Soil Amendment," Bulletin 1142, September 2, 2016, https://extension.uga .edu/publications/detail.html?number=B1142&title=best -management-practices-for-wood-ash-as-agricultural-soil -amendment.

2. See Arthur Schopenhauer, "On the Sufferings of the World," in *Studies in Pessimism*, trans. T. Bailey Saunders (London: Swan Sonnenschein, 1851), 1–28.

3. W. E. Sangster, "When Hope Is Dead, Hope On!" News for Christians, accessed June 6, 2024, https://www .newsforchristians.com/clser1/sangster003.html.

Chapter 10

1. Martyn Lloyd-Jones, *Joy Unspeakable: Power and Renewal in the Holy Spirit*, ed. Christopher Catherwood (Wheaton, IL: Harold Shaw, 1994), 18.

2. Billy Graham, *The Holy Spirit* (Nashville: W Publishing Group, 1978), vii.